Sailing Craft

of

East Anglia

Sailing Craft

of

East Anglia

ROGER FINCH and HERVEY BENHAM

with illustrations by Roger Finch

TERENCE DALTON LIMITED
LAVENHAM, SUFFOLK 1987

Published by
TERENCE DALTON LIMITED
ISBN 0 86138 049 5

Text photoset in 10/11pt Baskerville

Printed in Great Britain at
The Lavenham Press Limited, Lavenham, Suffolk

Contents

Preface

THIS book is the result of a life-long interest in the sailing craft of East Anglia shared by the joint authors and deepened by much lively discussion and exchanged ideas between themselves and others. Each has followed his especial line of interest in a richly diverse subject.

Besides providing line drawings Roger Finch has contributed those parts relating to trading under sail, while Hervey Benham has made his province the sections on fishing, fishing craft and methods and the current restoration and sailing of traditional working craft. This phenomenon has reintroduced to the scene the scent of stockholm tar and the sound of the caulking mallet, and has forestalled any danger of our study becoming remote and academic. Nowhere along the coast of Britain has this resurgence of traditional sailing craft taken place and been pursued with so much skill, enthusiasm and continued momentum as in the area which is the subject of this book. As one of its

originators, Hervey Benham is in the position to record its achievements with authority.

Both keen East Coast amateur sailors, we have for many years been forced to consider tides, winds and anchorages, the swatchways and channels much as the coasters did in the past. Such considerations, limited as they must be for those who sail in the second half of the twentieth century, do much to provide essential insight into the everyday life of the men who sailed and worked the craft recorded in these pages, men whose representatives have contributed so much to authenticate and enliven our account.

For Essex and Suffolk we have relied on a lifetime of shared experience with a host of friends almost too numerous to mention, though we must make an exception in the case of Colin Fox, Graham Hussey and John Leather, who has contributed from his wide personal knowledge as well as through his own published work, notably on Colchester smacks and Yarmouth shrimpers.

For Norfolk and the Wash, less familiar to us and less researched and documented, at King's Lynn we are grateful to J. R. Aldous (Clerk and Chief Fishery Officer of Eastern Sea Fisheries Joint Committee), Frank Castleton, David Howard, Jim Jude, and J. W. Worfolk; at Brancaster Staithe to Leonard Loose; at Fosdyke to Harry Lineham; and at Boston to Ron Worracker.

Finally we would like gratefully to acknowledge the sympathetic criticism and encouragement of Robert Malster of Terence Dalton, whose own wide knowledge of the subject is generally respected.

Opposite: The schooners *Commerce* and *Ellis* unloading coal on the open beach at Cromer. The last such cargo was landed at Cromer in 1876.   *Robert Malster*

Right: The spritsail barge *Lord Roberts*, built at Maldon in 1900, lying beside Stambridge mill at the head of the River Roach. Owned by the miller, she and her consort, the *Joy*, were sold to become yacht barges in the nineteen-sixties.
Roger Finch

Introduction 1

THESE pages and the illustrations which accompany the text are devoted to celebrating and recording the last generation of the sailing craft of East Anglia. We have restricted our studies to a period roughly encompassing the half-century prior to the end of the First World War; that is to say, the decades immediately before the revolution wrought by the adoption of the internal combustion engine, both afloat and ashore, produced such profound changes to our way of life. If we have made excursions beyond these self-imposed limitations it is because we feel they help to illuminate the story. This is particularly true of the account of the sailing barges, for some of the finest spritties launched on the East Coast were not built until the nineteen-twenties, and their red sails were still to be seen at sea until a decade or more after the Second World War. We also record the brave efforts of those who, with exemplary energy and devotion, restore and save traditional craft of every sort which would otherwise have been lost for ever.

The traditional sailing craft of East Anglia had been honed and shaped over the centuries to serve their masters along a coast and on rivers which have a demanding variety. There is the southerly world of shallow tidal waters, sinuous creeks, inlets and rivers. Much of this low-lying coast is artificial, delineated by continuous sea walls which could never have been built without the help of sailing barges and their predecessors bringing stone for their construction and maintenance. Northwards of the River Orwell there are more tidal rivers, but less easy of access, and here a shelving shingle beach faces the sea. This beach, scored with storm ridges, continues until we almost reach the furthest boundary of East Anglia. Along the North Norfolk coast there are lonely salt marshes, ancient forgotten ports and mudflats, until the watery wastes of the Wash are reached. Midway along the coast line, the Broads meet the sea, a uniquely man-made region of waterways and lakes. Every one of these regions stamped a distinctive character on its trading and fishing craft, and among the latter could be found vessels designed to gather every harvest the sea had to offer from oysters to cod.

At the point where the estuaries could be bridged there had grown up such ports as Maldon on the Blackwater, Ipswich on the Orwell, and Wisbech on the

The last commercial square-rigger to discharge at Ipswich, the *Abraham Rydberg*, with the spritsail barges *May* and *Kimberley* alongside, 1938.   *Arthur Bennett*

Nene. These man-made crossings effectively prevented a masted vessel from progressing further upstream, and from Saxon times stimulated the growth of bridge settlements into ports. Their merchants tended to develop specialised craft which could lighter cargoes beyond the bridges along winding waterways such as the Stour, whose river trade carried in distinctive clinker-built barges was immortalised by John Constable. In 1986 the site of a dry dock, familiar to those who know the artist's painting *Barge-building near Flatford Mill*, was excavated. Beneath the silt on the brick bottom of the dock was discovered the remains of one such vessel.

The Broadlands especially bred its own characteristic sailing lighter, the black-sailed wherry, which also extended navigation up the Blyth above Blythburgh and made Halesworth an inland port. A few spritsail barges worked both about the estuary of the Orwell and above bridges on the river Gipping, but for the rest the river craft were towed or poled.

As seagoing vessels were built with an increasing draft, the older tidal ports found themselves relegated for use by out-dated craft, survivors of the days of wood and hemp, but no less interesting for that. Some of the oldest bridge ports have quietly decayed. Red-tiled warehouses and maltings, wooden tidal quays, the channels to them marked only with gaunt withies, all speak of a former prosperity. There is Snape which once had its own shipyard and Blythburgh, where the wherry *Star of Halesworth*, last of all the fine argosies which had moored at its quay below the bridge, discharged its final cargo in 1906. From all these ports and many others, flour and malt, both products of locally grown grain, were transported to Thamesside bakeries and breweries under sail within living memory, while English wheat and flour left Ipswich for the Pool of London and the Medway in the holds of sailing barges in the nineteen-fifties.

Easily dug sand on land close to the shores of the River Colne at first provided ballast for the round-bottomed brigs and schooners and then a stream of paying cargoes for the barges. Brickearth and clay, discovered close by the banks of rivers and creeks from the Alde southwards, encouraged the establishment of brickyards from Tudor times onwards. Shipping away their production and bringing fuel for their kilns kept sailing craft busy until well into the twentieth century.

Some of our sailing craft hailed from ports which were established without such a sure and certain foundation as the bridge ports for their prosperity. Two of these, Harwich and Lowestoft, have paid for it by a continuing economic uncertainty, aggravated by their having to wage a lengthy war of attrition against an alliance of the sea and the north wind. The dominant wind (the one which blows with the greatest force) on the East Coast is a northerly one. While this has the advantage of providing a sheltered shore from Leigh to Lowestoft for those putting to sea, or more likely seeking a safe anchorage, northerly gales indirectly produce the coast's most distinctive maritime features. The turbulence that gale force winds produce causes a continual southerly drift of vast quantities of sand and shingle, eroded from the soft rocks of the shore line, scores great parallel furrows in the sea bed and builds up long ridges of sand offshore. It also creates long southerly-pointing fingers of waterborne material which threaten to strangle the entrances of the estuaries, barring or severely limiting the passage of shipping.

The offshore sands, frequently changing their outline and always producing a tumbling chaos of sea during gales, were deathtraps for the huge fleets of sailing colliers and timber carriers bound for London. The shores facing the sands produced the finest salvagers' beach boats and the Essex cruising smacks besides the staunchest class of sailing lifeboat to be found anywhere around the coast of Britain. The R.N.L.I. reported in 1852 that they strongly advocated that lifeboats should be rowed but that "the Yarmouth, Lowestoft, Southwold and Deal boatmen are so skilful in the management of their boats that they perhaps form an exception" and could use sails. But as well as creating hidden hazards, the shallow banks gave shelter where the huge shoals of sprats could congregate for the stowboaters from the Colne and Blackwater to harvest, herrings for the "luggers" to net in autumn, and shallower water for long-lining and trawling under sail, using a multitude of craft and rigs.

Along East Anglia's northern-facing shore and Norfolk's smooth forehead, the full power of the dominant northerly wind also tends to produce long sandy spits, but trending in an easterly direction, and to accumulate wide expanses of clean sand in front of the low cliffs. The sands provide ideal conditions for the growth of a wide range of crustacaea, and consequentially a distinctive form of beach boat to exploit them. The level sands made it possible for little sailing ships to put themselves ashore at high water to discharge their cargoes of coal, tiles

A beach yawl awaiting the call.

Wells quay in Edwardian days, with steamers and a ketch-rigged billyboy. *Robert Malster*

and bricks into locally conscripted horse-drawn tumbrils for the benefit of the remote communities beyond the sand dunes. But no deep-water harbours could grow up there and it remains even to this day a remote and lonely shore.

Further along the coast the same powerful natural forces which accumulated the sands for the crabs and shellfish to multiply upon almost strangled the little ports of Cley, Blakeney and Wells. The tidal action which yearly shallowed the entrance to their quays was aggravated by the enclosing of the adjacent marshes by land reclaimers from the early seventeenth to the late nineteenth centuries. Gradually these harbours were forsaken by all but the most persistent seagoing traders such as the billyboys, ketch barges, spritties and Dutch tjalks, which did not seem to worry overmuch if the antique equipment for discharging and loading their modest cargoes belonged to an even earlier age than they did themselves and that the tides might delay them for weeks.

Yarmouth, as ancient as the North Norfolk ports which had been throttled by a combination of winds and sand, turned the long shingle spit which had formed at its front door into the foundation for a majestic quay which Defoe congratulated the inhabitants upon, describing it as one of the finest in Europe. From the port of Yarmouth sailed fleets of herring drifters and the smacks to reap a reward from the North Sea. Nearby is Lowestoft, another fishing station equally popular for the herring drifters and the smacks in the days of sail, and the very last harbour at which sailing trawlers landed their catch. It was, in contrast to Yarmouth, an upstart among East Anglian ports, and very nearly suffered an early demise as a penalty for its insolence. Only persistent and costly engineering kept the harbour entrance free from choking shingle, remorselessly piled up by each winter's northerly gales. A little to the south, an attempt to revive the ancient port of Southwold at the beginning of our century to provide a refuge for the sailing fishing craft crowded out from Lowestoft was ultimately frustrated for the same reason. While we write it is threatened with becoming unusable, even as a haven for the little fleet of inshore fishermen which uses its quay at Blackshore on the Blyth. Yet it was here, in days gone by, that herring drifters moored while boomie barges and schooners tied up with cargoes to be lightered inland as far as the maltings at Halesworth.

During the years encompassed by our story, all these craft enjoyed the kindly disposed south-west wind which blew more frequently than any other. South-westerly gales, when they do blow up, are shortlived, and East Anglia suffers fewer gales than any other part of the British coastline, allowing more days for seamen to work under sail, either fishing or trading along the shore. While the north-west wind was the coaster's favourite between London and Harwich, a voyage in smooth water in both directions, the south-westerlies gave the inshore fishermen from Kessingland down to the Orwell an offshore wind for their work and the chance to beach their boats in the evening with the minimum danger from the surf, for it is said in East Anglia "Sun go down, wind go down".

The prevailing south-westerly breeze gave a good chance to the skipper of a schooner or brigantine when he was negotiating the channel of an East Anglian river, for most run from north-west to south-east, and it was a beam wind for the sailing trawlers bound for the North Sea fishing grounds. Within the last decade or so these hitherto prevailing south-westerlies have for some inexplicable reason failed. There is now a greater tendency for northerlies to predominate, although only the weekend amateur sailor is left to bemoan the change.

But winds have always been uncertain and unpredictable; in the days of sail, fishermen and bargemen were equally concerned with the tides, which were a certainty. The tidal streams were kindly disposed for passage making, for a vessel working towards London, generally against a headwind, enjoyed the benefit of seven hours' flood tide; and though a vessel bound northwards could only rely on five hours' ebb, it usually had the compensation of a fair wind.

The range of the tide on the East Coast is a useful one and, except perhaps when it comes racing in across the flat sands of the North Norfolk coast, it has no spite in it. It gives the shipwright a reasonable chance to work on a craft that the flood tide has conveniently lifted on to the wooden blocks of the riverside shipyard. It powered the tidemills on the creeks and rivers of the southern shore below the Deben which supplied cargoes for sailing barges and ketches. The fact that the tidal range at Yarmouth is only eight feet must have helped to recommend the port to traders and fishermen alike, for it caused them the minimum of inconvenience in tending the warps and mooring lines as they lay in their scores alongside the quay. The careless navigator of the East Coast tideways is deposited upon the dry mud all too easily, but if he is then exposed to ridicule, at least he is not endangered, for there is no fierce tide scouring away the bank under his bilge to topple him over, though the hard and dangerous sands of the Thames Estuary are another matter. They caused so many wrecks that "salvaging" became an important part of many fishermen's lives and even a full-time occupation before the introduction of the lifeboats and steam tugs. There were nevertheless cases of sailing barges cast up high and dry after an estuary gale, only to be refloated down a temporary slipway, little the worse for the experience.

The fact that she traded to tidal ports helped to prolong the commercial viability of the sailing barge trading along the East Coast. Her motor-driven equivalent, in defiance of wind and weather, might well arrive at its destination while the sailorman was still laboriously turning to windward, only to find that it could not come alongside a tidal quay until there was sufficient water.

Few East Coast working craft performed well enough to windward to tackle a tide which was not in their favour, together with a head wind. The family of barge-built sailing craft all carried leeboards in order to make any work to windward at all possible, and sensibly they invariably waited for a fair tide to commence a passage. The most weatherly working boats were probably the bigger Colne smacks; even they could only sail within rather less than five points (some fifty degrees) of the wind's direction; that was only achieved under moderate conditions of wind and sea. However, the comparative weatherliness of individual working craft was a constant source of lively discussion among the men who sailed them, and it has been left to the restorers of working craft in our own day to attempt to provide a more objective assessment, although the arguments are no less heated.

A man who went to sea for his living under sail certainly wanted a weatherly vessel, but was as much concerned with his smack providing a safe and convenient working platform, or his barge being a commodious cargo carrier. The first tended to prefer a fishing craft with a low profile aft to assist his handling of the nets, while the estuary traders developed huge hatches and boxy lines so that their skippers could persuade dockers to stow the largest cargoes below decks easily and economically. The variety and idiosyncrasies of the craft we record were all the result of evolution over the centuries, dictated by environment and purpose, limited by the materials and techniques available to their builders and the pockets of their owners.

As far as the men who sailed them were concerned, fishing and trading were, to a great extent, separate and distinct ways of life. A seaman who was unable to find a berth aboard a coasting schooner might sign on for a deep-sea voyage, but few smacksmen shipped in a sailing barge or sailormen in a trawling smack and there were self-contained communities of fishermen living along the Rows at Yarmouth and on the Denes at Lowestoft where few except they and their families would venture. The fisheries themselves divided into a range of widely differing trades and techniques, hardly less exclusive than the division

The spritsail barge *Hyacinth* of Maldon, built there by Howard in 1889 and owned by Bentall. Her refined transom was a hallmark of her builder. *Hervey Benham*

between fishermen and merchant seamen. Some of these techniques have been described in detail in other books; some have hardly been recorded. For this reason, we have dealt with a few of the minor fisheries more fully than others which were perhaps more important but are already familiar to the reader.

The variety and interest of the local craft, fishing and freighting between the Wash and the Thames Estuary, were unequalled around the whole British coastline, perhaps throughout Europe. The tradition also persisted longer than elsewhere. Smacks were trawling out of Lowestoft until 1939, and oyster dredging under sail continued in Essex until the Second World War. Throughout the nineteen-fifties, Ipswich was the last home of the final survivors of sail, the sailing barge, until the *Anglia* and *Marjorie* were sold to become barge-yachts in 1960, leaving only the *Cambria* a regular trader to Yarmouth, until she too ceased trading and was acquired by the Maritime Trust in 1970. For these reasons, our account of so many craft, so various in their form and their purpose, has an interest far beyond the region we describe.

Nineteenth-century traders; a small cutter and a ketch-rigged billyboy dried out at low water.

Traders and Trading Days

SAIL lasted longer on the East Coast than anywhere else in north-western Europe. At the end of the Second World War, there still remained some two hundred spritsail sailing barges actively trading between the Humber and the Thames. Even this notable fleet was but a shadow of a former glory, for trade under sail had been an integral part of the fabric of trade on the East Anglian coast for centuries. It had brought prosperity in the days when the wool trade made East Anglia one of the wealthiest regions of Britain. Later, when the centre of gravity of trade moved away from the borders of the North Sea to the Western Approaches, and with the coming of iron ships and steam power shipbuilding became concentrated on the north-east and north-west coasts, sail still retained its importance. The ports and tidal harbours and even the open beaches saw the coming and going of a multiplicity of sailing craft which, if they no longer represented the most modern or efficient of seaborne carriers, lacked nothing in interest or diversity.

For our present purpose we will look no further back in time than the moment when with the coming of the railway a revolution took place. The transportation of materials and foodstuffs was then no longer a monopoly of river and seaborne trade. Yet the sailing craft which survived from that period disappeared only slowly; a few lasted, surviving generations of technical change, into our own century, to be recorded by the camera and accurately documented. They belonged to a world that was rapidly passing even when they were launched, a world which linked them with a distant past.

By the eighteen-sixties the time when ocean traders were built on a small enough scale to be owned at ports such as Colchester, Ipswich, Yarmouth, Wells and King's Lynn had all but gone. It was no longer possible for an East Anglian shipowner to order a brig or brigantine from the local shipyard, find four or five like-minded venturers to take up a proportion of the sixty-four shares into which, by tradition, the necessary capital was divided, and show a profit on the investment.

Although Harvey at Wivenhoe had given up building commercial vessels by then, as late as the eighteen-seventies and eighties Vaux's yard at Harwich, Bayley's at Ipswich, and Fellows' at Yarmouth were all launching vessels intended for deep-water trading, but they were rarely for local buyers. By this time, the twin poles of Hull and London were drawing to themselves to an ever-increasing extent the ocean-going tonnage which imported the raw materials and food-grains in bulk required by an industrialised nation. However, the necessary redistribution of this along the East Coast, costly to undertake by rail, created a whole new generation of sailing craft as rich in its character as the small deep-water vessels which were now relegated to a less heroic existence, usually in the coal trade. The middle of the nineteenth century saw 585 merchant sailing ships owned at Yarmouth. Many were colliers or vessels relegated to the coal trade in their old age; the last of the breed, the brigantine *Hannah*, built there in 1794, was lost off Winterton in 1907 carrying coals.

While the coal trade from the North had, as far as the Metropolis was concerned, been captured by the highly systematised use of steam ships, returning in ballast to the coal ports in a matter of days, the delivery of black diamonds all along the coast from Boston to Leigh on the Thames relied on a motley gathering of wooden brigs, brigantines and schooners. Their only common denominator was the fact that they had been originally rigged for deepsea work, and many had commenced their career highly classed at Lloyd's for carrying valuable cargoes. The fine craftsmanship and materials put into their construction stood them in good stead as they eked out a precarious existence with grimy canvas set from masts shorn of their former glory. If they were lucky they secured a return cargo of scrap metal, wheat, or oats for the pit ponies. Occasionally they would take coal to the small northern French ports, despised by the steamers for the antique discharging equipment they used.

Much of the timber, and ice for the North Sea fishery before the days of cheap refrigeration, was brought from Scandinavia to the East Coast ports on

With her mainsail reefed to clear the deck cargo of timber, the spritsail barge *Centaur* makes her way along Sea Reach on the Thames.   *Hervey Benham*

Lowestoft South Quay in the nineties: Scandinavian square-riggers unload timber from the Baltic, a sailing barge brings in a cargo of deals from London and wherries load general cargoes.

H. Jenkins

vessels which were owned around the shores of the Baltic. Nevertheless an alternative to coal drudging was for the East Coast brigs and brigantines to make a summertime venture to Oslo and return with deck cargoes of deal for the Victorian house-building boom. Yarmouth and Lowestoft were traditionally the ports to which most of the timber-carriers returned, for the fishing industry had an insatiable demand for softwoods, barrel staves and mast timber. Timber-carrying Baltic schooners and barquentines could still be found discharging alongside the quays at Yarmouth immediately before the opening of the Second World War. Norfolk wherries regularly loaded direct from them, piling the deals on deck above the hatches and cantilevered out over the sides, and sometimes towing rafts of timber astern, bound for Norwich. The last foreign traders to Woodbridge, winding their way up the Deben, were Norwegian brigantines loaded with deals.

Timber came in indirectly to other ports along the East Anglian coast by spritsail barge. The cargoes were loaded in the London docks, usually in the

autumn. Once the hold was filled a deck cargo was piled several feet high above the hatches and secured with chains and wires. Then, with the mainsail and foresail reefed to clear the stack of timber, the barge would set sail for a quay at Maldon, Manningtree or Ipswich.

Maldon, although the only port on the Blackwater to have built seagoing merchantmen and latterly barges, had been upstaged by Heybridge lower down the river. Here a connection with Chelmsford had been made by a canalised river. Into the canal basin, half way along Colliers Reach, came a steady trade of coal and timber, carried first by brigs and then by brigantines and finally by ketch barges and spritties. The last square-riggers to be seen were the Scandinavians in with poles and lumber, first discharging part of their cargo by lighter or sailing barge to enable them to float over the relatively shallow sill of the lock.

The greatest number of spritties were employed in the farmyard-trade which was unique to the region. Sailing stacks of straw, hay and kindling into the heart of London was a trade centuries old, but by the nineteenth century the growth of the Great Wen was such that it demanded a steady stream of fodder and bedding for its thousands of horses. Essex barges did most of the work, and the London hay and straw markets relied upon them for their supplies, while the stable owners depended upon the barges for the removal of the stable sweepings, which were returned to enrich the land of the farms whence the hay had come. Although the Blackwater and the Colne supplied most, cargoes of straw and hay were loaded from quays on the Stour, the Orwell and the Deben. The last such cargo was shipped in 1935 from Erwarton on the Stour, where the sad stumps of the rotted wooden quay can still be seen.

This was only one of a dozen different cargoes which employed the sailing barges. They distributed imported grain cargoes from the huge freighters in the London docks to the mills, maltings and breweries along the East Coast. It was a hard trade, for it meant that wooden sailing barges, dependent upon sail alone, had to face a dockland world of steel, concrete and machinery in order to secure a cargo. Its compensations were the passage to be made once clear of the shipping in the Thames, and then a quiet berth beside a wooden quay at Saltcote on the Blackwater, at Mistley on the Stour, at Woodbridge, or at an almost forgotten inland port such as Snape or Beccles. Cement from the Medway came to Lowestoft and the raw materials for artificial fertiliser to Ipswich. When there was a cement works at Waldringfield barges brought chalk from the Thames and Medway for the works; others went "mudding" in the Deben.

Originating from the industrialised Humber, a similar redistribution trade, although on a rather less extensive scale, took place. Little craft, quite unlike the spritsail barges, loaded coal at Goole, or took aboard cargoes at the numerous

A trading cutter and a clinker-built billyboy dried out at Woodbridge in the days before the spritsail barge dominated the scene. The tide mill can be seen in the background of this photograph, taken in 1858.
Suffolk Photographic Survey

13

Humberside quays from steamers loaded with cattle food or from the riverside brick and tile makers on the southern shore. These were sailed to now half-forgotten ports along the North Norfolk coast, occasionally further south to the Deben and Orwell, while building stone from Yorkshire for Victorian churches and town halls was always in demand.

Many of these craft, whose outward appearance had changed little since the eighteenth century, were of the traditional Humber build, although they traded far afield and were an accepted part of the East Anglian waterside scene. They were known as billyboys; perhaps their name derived from the eighteenth-century coasting vessels known as bilanders, a vessel which sailed "by the land". Whether this is correct or not, it certainly describes the trading limitations of these little craft. They perpetuated the eighteenth-century convention of referring to a vessel's hull form in order to identify it, rather than its rig. Whether rigged as sloops, cutters, ketches or schooners, to the East Coast seamen they were billyboys.

As well as these rotund craft the Humber coasting fleet included several smart schooners of a more conventional mould. Together with the billyboys and fishing smacks made redundant by the introduction of steam trawlers at Grimsby and the north-east fishing ports and converted to cargo carrying, they were to be found in most East Anglian harbours and ports, including Norwich, until well into the twentieth century. Unlike the barges they could not go to sea without ballast, but fortunately shingle for dock construction was in constant demand and readily available. Often seen on the Deben, they would discharge their cargoes at Woodbridge and then stagger down to Bawdsey and load a stiffening from the beach.

Besides yards on the Humber, where the ones at Knottingley were the most prolific, the billyboys were launched at Lynn and Wells. At Wells the yards owned by Tyrell and Joseph Springall, both of whom had constructed brigs in

the eighteen-fifties, built them. The most southerly yard to launch a billyboy was one at Woodbridge which built the *Monarch* in 1839, traditionally planked part carvel and part clinker.

It may be a source of wonder that in a world that was becoming increasingly served by mechanised transport, sail could have survived for so long. The explanation was that to build a steamer small enough to shift bulk cargoes, similar to those carried by a barge or ketch, had been shown to be unprofitable. Overheads of insurance, engineer's wages and the cost of fuel all contributed to make it uneconomic to employ a small steam-powered vessel to deliver a cargo to a port where the vessel might idle for weeks. Merchants used to the ways of sail had a tendency to treat ships as a cheap form of warehousing, while a return cargo might be days accumulating. Moreover, the tidal berths in which the steamer might lie, drying out at low tide, were capable of causing damage and putting capital at risk.

These factors preserved a regular trade to the west coast harbours of Ireland in flour, malt and artificial fertilisers and the chance of a return cargo of oats. This was reserved for the last round-bottomed schooners owned at Yarmouth and Ipswich. They were prepared to wait upon the inevitable delays in unloading and loading which steamers would not tolerate, while unlike the ketch barges they were built and rigged to withstand Atlantic gales.

But steamers had captured one sector of the small sailing vessel's traditional trade by the eighteen-eighties. For centuries fast, weatherly and well-found craft of a small tonnage had shuttled back and forth between the quays on the Pool of London and the East Anglian ports to as regular a timetable as wind and weather permitted. There were also long-established regular services to Gainsborough on the Trent and to Hull. Ports north of Yarmouth looked primarily to these as a destination of their packet sloops and maintained a long-lasting service to the Humber. The little *Blakeney and Hull Packet* sailed from Wells, partnered by the

Opposite: King's Lynn in the days when billyboys and other small vessels lay at moorings in the Ouse. At right can be seen the spars of a small brig in the entrance to the River Nar.
Robert Malster

Right: Two billyboys lying moored head and stern to buoys in the Ouse at King's Lynn. The nearer one is the *Evening Star* of Hull, built at Mexborough in 1873.   *Robert Malster*

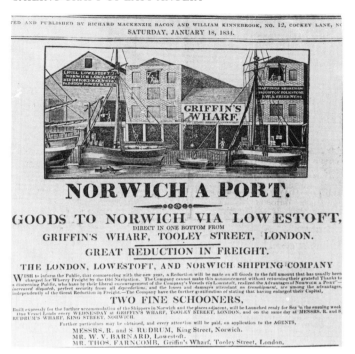

Left: An advertisement dated 1834 for a regular service of traders between London, Lowestoft and Norwich. *Robert Malster*

Opposite: A typical schooner employed in the coastal and continental trade, the *Pride of Mistley* of Harwich is seen in a painting dated 1866.
Roger Finch

London Packet, until the sixties. They carried miscellaneous cargoes (and the occasional passengers) which, even after the coming of the railways, were still transported by water. Groceries and lamp oil, Coade stone statues from Lambeth and barrelled beer from the City, iron cooking pots and zinc baths were all distributed in this way. At first the trade was carried by smart round-bottomed sloops, cutters and the occasional schooner. Later, from the southerly ports crack spritsail barges, whose sailing times were well advertised in the local press, and whose arrivals were timed to link with the carrier's cart, were used. The carrier's cart, in a pre-motorised age, joined the ports and havens with the inland villages.

It was a lucrative trade, if a demanding one. Valuable cargoes of malt and corn for City brewers and distillers supplied regular outward cargoes for the Thames. It was not surprising that by the eighties the trade had been captured by miniature steamers, which could guarantee a regular arrival and which were almost as characterful as the sailing hoys they replaced. Only lamp-oil remained a cargo for sail to carry, as it was considered too potentially dangerous for rail or the steamers, and was regularly carried until the First World War.

Elsewhere, the small scale of much nineteenth-century rural industry, which did not worry overmuch about its delivery dates, was admirably suited to employ the sailing barge and its variants. There were brick fields at Shoeburyness, on Brightlingsea creek, on the Stour, at the entrance to the Deben and on the banks

of the Alde, to name a few. All these and many others were served by barges and
billyboys. There were waterside mills and maltings everywhere, on the
Blackwater, at Mistley, at Beccles and on Oulton Broad. All provided cargoes for
barges; some owned their own fleets, while bargeowners could secure long-term
contracts which at Mistley encouraged the building of steel spritsail barges until
the nineteen-thirties.

Of the hundreds of remote inland wharfs used for centuries by sail only a
very few are still active. At Battlesbridge, at the navigable head of the Essex
Crouch, the mill once owned its own schooner and is still served by water.
Similarly, on the Broomhill River tributary of the Roach, the mill at Stambridge
continued to run its own sailing barges until the nineteen-fifties and now has
motor craft working to it. Another winding creek, off the Colne, enables craft to
reach the mill at Fingringhoe as they have done for centuries, although now
diesels assist in the navigation. In Suffolk the only working survival of a tidal
wharf for trade is at Snape, on the Alde. Occasionally motor coasters seek out the
quay by the maltings, where once a steady trade under sail came and went, and a
schooner-barge was built.

For the rest, a few have been kept alive as a base for yachtsmen,
pre-eminently Pin Mill on the Orwell where coals were discharged from boomies
on the long hard and the stone-dredgers' smacks used to anchor where the
yachts are moored today. Other hards and quays are barely accessible today even

by a dinghy. Among the lonely archipelago of the Essex islands there are Landwick and Millhead, where it is recorded that on one occasion twenty sprits could be counted above the creek-walls, belonging to the barges which served the brickworks there.

Off the River Blackwater Old Hall Creek, near Tollesbury, had a busy wharf at its head a century ago which has disappeared, and close by no more barges will reach Salcot, for the creek is now dammed. There were another half-dozen landings on the Blackwater, among them Bradwell (which had its own barge fleet) and Lawling for hay barges and Heybridge for malt and barley. Off the Colne it is easy to imagine that the creeks leading to St Osyth were busy ones, serving the maltings and the tidemill, but less easy to believe that little coasters were launched there in the early nineteenth century. Not far away barges served the mill at Thorrington at the head of Alresford Creek.

Leaving the Colne and going further north we come to the Walton Backwaters, a network of creeks and saltings. There were busy wharfs at

Opposite: The little schooner *Bee* discharging coal in the tidemill dock at Walton-on-Naze. She regularly carried bagged flour on the return trip to the North. The *Bee* was eventually lost when driven ashore in an easterly gale at Withernsea, Yorkshire.
Roger Finch

Left: A sailing barge makes it way down the Colne with a stack of straw for the Kent paper mills during a short-lived resurgence of the stackie trade just after the Second World War.
Roger Finch

Beaumont—only a persistent dinghy sailor would reach there today—
Landermere and Kirby. Coal came in by sail to what is now the yacht club hard at
Walton and flour went north by sail from the nearby tidemill, demolished in
1921.

Before the modern port developments existed on the Stour there was a dock
on a creek which led off the main stream behind Dovercourt, although this had
been partly closed in the eighteenth century. There were quays and hards at
Shotley Gate for coal, at Erwarton for straw and hay and at the head of Holbrook
creek for bricks from the nearby yard. Above the bridge at Cattawade the mill
quay at Brantham has gone with the mill, and now nothing larger than a boat can
reach where once spritsail barges loaded.

Moving on to the grander Orwell, there were besides Pin Mill several
barge-landings. Probably the most important was at the head of Levington
Creek, which saw its last barge in 1940, and from where two centuries before the
first cargoes of red crag for fertiliser were loaded. On the opposite shore Hares
Creek and Frog Alley were popular with stackie barges. Further upstream
Redgate hard, close by Freston Tower, was well used for farm work.

The head of navigation on the Deben is Wilford Bridge. The quay, still
there, was used by barges inward bound with roadstone, while lower downriver

the quay at Waldringfield, as has been mentioned elsewhere, originally served industry rather than yachtsmen. Ramsholt quay, unspoiled despite its popularity, was built as a wharf to load coprolites, red crag, and then hay. On the opposite shore, Kirton creek had its own somewhat grandiosely named "dock".

Boyton dock, where there is still a brick-built coal house standing lonely above the marshes, has its own wharf on the Butley river, leading off the Alde. Barges occasionally reached the head of the creek for cargoes from the mill. Much of the trade in the days of sail on this river related to the brickyard opposite Cob Island, where the remains of a pier may still be detected. It was associated with London brick companies and Smeed, Dean barges based in Kent were frequent visitors. Further up the Alde half a century earlier, a regular hoy service ran from a tiny dock at Iken, until recently just discernible among the reeds.

The quays on the Blyth, before the attempt at the beginning of the century to build a modern harbour, were at Blackshore, where schooners were built until

A tiller steered barge unloading "London mixture" for Suffolk farms at Waldringfield on the Deben. *Suffolk Photographic Survey.*

1848, and besides the keels and wherries, sea-going traders worked their way to a quay at Blythburgh bridge. Spritsail barges had penetrated as far north as the Blyth by the beginning of the nineteenth century and the last of the ketch barges brought roadstone to the newly-built quays in the nineteen-twenties.

At the old red-brick maltings on Oulton Broad only pleasure boats tie up where once barges and billyboys brought coal and barley and loaded malt. The first seagoing vessel to reach Beccles discharged her cargo of coal there in 1821, but the quay is unlikely to see again the sailing barges that delivered cargoes there as late as the nineteen-fifties. The trade to Norwich Riverside, despite the thirty-one miles of waterway which connect it with the sea, has been revived in this century. After the coming of the railways only smaller wooden coasting craft reached there, but of late short-sea traders are again regular visitors.

The Norfolk coast, where wheatfields stand within sight of the breakers, is without estuaries and therefore less rich in old quays. There is, nevertheless, evidence at Brancaster Staithe and Overy Staithe of a trade under sail. There the maltings and a granary still stand close to a tumbledown quay. There is no need to look far for proof of Blakeney's seaborne trade, although even relatively small vessels were forced to lighter out part of their cargo before tying up alongside the quay. Nearby Morston, once with its own quay, is today left to the seabirds. Cley has evidence of a past seaborne trade, but spritties never visited it, only the sloops and finally their billyboy successors. Hunstanton is said once to have had a jetty for landing coal but this was usually discharged at beach landings, such as

On the opposite page the miniature barge *Energy* is seen with a party of pleasure-seekers at Burnham-on-Crouch Regatta in 1907. *A. Pyner*

The barquentine *Elizabeth Stevens*, built in 1871 for Welsh owners, one of a series of barquentines launched at Ipswich from the yard of William Bayley for deep sea trading during the eighteen-seventies. This rig became popular at that period as a means of economising on running costs.   *Private collection*

those at Heacham and Cromer, although naturally they have left little evidence behind.

Beach landings were established only where there were suitable firm beaches and access through the dunes for the tumbrils to come down to the shore for loading with coal and occasionally to bring down corn. These approaches were known as gaps. Trimingham Gap, Walcott Gap, where there was a capstan to haul up the colliers and so give more time for the carters, and Horsey Gap are surviving names which record an ancient trade.

It would be unfair to conclude our voyage without reference to the Wash ports. Sutton Bridge, on the way to Wisbech, saw brigs and schooners in its day, but the abandoned dock there is now only a reminder of unrealised ambition. The Brinks at Wisbech were once crowded with every type of sailing barge and a fleet of deep-sea square-riggers was owned there. Fosdyke Bridge on the Welland is now the home of a few fishing boats, but it once had a coasting trade which was still carried on by auxiliary sailing barges until after the Second World War.

It would be foolish to romanticise the life of the men who worked aboard the sailing coasters and smacks. However, when it is compared with the impoverished existence of the East Anglian farm labourer or the grinding toil of a worker in the quayside maltings at the beginning of the twentieth century, their lot had at least an element of variety and encouraged an independent turn of mind. When at sea life was lived in a roughly egalitarian manner.

Its material rewards were meagre enough, although it was possible with luck and application for a boy-cook to rise to a position of command. It was expected that a youngster whose family had financial interests in shipping, either fishing or trading, entered the profession through the hawser hole and not the cabin companionway. An example, carefully documented by his descendant, is the career of John Brown of East Donyland, on the Essex Colne, who in 1838 at the age of fifteen joined the smack *Rival* as an indentured apprentice. She was a veteran built at Wivenhoe in 1757 and had been involved in smuggling, an incident which led to her seizure and auction by the Court of Exchequer in 1797. He soon transferred to the larger nineteen-ton smack *Henry Elizabeth* of Colchester, owned at John's birthplace and employed dredging septaria stone off the Essex coast and landing it at Harwich for the manufacture of cement. On the completion of his apprenticeship on the smack, John made a number of

The brig *Tweedside* of Cley, which in the eighteen-sixties was a port of registration, refitting at Wisbech. Owned by Porrit of Cley, she is typical of the many brigs owned on the East Coast during the middle decades of the nineteenth century; her copper sheathing indicates that she was intended for deep sea trading.   *Roger Finch*

Left: The entrance to Yarmouth harbour, with a West Country schooner and a Yarmouth smack towing out behind one of the local paddle tugs. *Nautical Photo Agency*

Opposite: The harbour at Blakeney, with the billyboy ketch *Blue Jacket* and the ex-trawler *Fiducia*; on the extreme right is a steel billyboy cutter. The two lighters were used by vessels too deeply laden to come over the bar. *Roger Finch*

voyages in the Home Trade as a seaman aboard his uncle Joseph's ninety-four ton schooner *Banff*. Coal was the principal cargo, loaded at Newcastle and Middlesbrough and discharged at the East Coast ports. When his uncle was appointed to command the bigger schooner *Leader* of Ipswich he followed him. Rated as an able seaman, he was judged capable of standing his trick at the wheel unsupervised and reeving a topsail stuns'l halyard aloft, skills which earned him three pounds a month and all food found.

A voyage aboard the *Leader*, outward bound with coal to the Black Sea and returning with grain, which lasted almost six months gave John a taste of foreign seas. Upon his return he was granted his mate's certificate at the age of twenty-one, and by the eighteen-fifties, like many other keen youngsters, he had transferred his allegiance to steam and was accepted as mate on one of the new steam colliers. He only served once again for a short spell in sail and rose to a position of command in 1870, taking charge of the pioneer steam collier *John Bowes*, which by then was something of an out-dated veteran.

Such a successful maritime career, after a hard grounding as an apprentice under sail, was only open to those who possessed a good basic education and could take advantage of family connections, but it is nevertheless a typical one. At the fishing ports of Lowestoft and Yarmouth where a rapid expansion presented increased opportunities a flair for finding fish at sea and landing it fresh was valued above any other qualifications for those who sought to secure a skipper's berth. Prior to 1883, it was unnecessary for the skipper or mate of a

smack to hold a Board of Trade certificate. After that date, an oral examination was instituted, which assessed the candidate's knowledge of the rule of the road at sea and his ability to deal with the practical emergencies that could occur on the fishing grounds. Subsequently, more testing written examinations were introduced, banishing the table-top models which, in order to illustrate their answers, the candidates had manoeuvred under the critical eyes of the examiner. However, most of those who skippered the last of the sailing trawlers had learned and were examined in the hard school of experience.

Lowestoft was traditionally the port of skipper-owners or family-owned groups of smacks. Yarmouth tended to be the base for large company-owned fleets, with a resulting hardening of relationships between owners and crew. Unlike some others, the crews of Hewett's fleet based at Gorleston benefited from an unusual paternalism. It employed some five hundred men in its heyday, owned company houses and a hospital founded expressly for the treatment of injured fishermen. It was at the suggestion of the manager of the Short Blue fleet, as Hewett's was known, that in 1881 the Mission to Deep Sea Fishermen fitted out a specially equipped smack providing much-needed medical and surgical aid on the fishing grounds.

Most of the smack skippers began as boy-cooks. This was a designation bestowed upon a fourteen-year-old lad who had placed his foot on the first rung of the ladder of promotion. For a modest seven shillings a week, he coiled down the trawl warp below decks, generally assisted in the working of the vessel and

25

prepared food for the crew. His wage is placed in perspective when we remember that the one hundredweight of potatoes he peeled each week cost two shillings and sixpence; the bacon he fried, on Sundays only, was sixpence per pound, while meat was almost as cheap. If his knowledge of cooking was limited, he learned by doing, preparing the salt beef, stored in the harness casks, together with the suet for grating into the puddings, an essential item of diet and only occasionally enlivened with treacle or raisins.

Aboard merchantmen, the harness cask, a brass-bound oak barrel, was securely padlocked and the key held in the captain's possession. While pay and conditions varied from port to port in both smacks and schooners, it was usual that the ship fed the crew and, by contemporary working-class standards ashore, well. Basic pay for a smack skipper was fourteen shillings per week, plus one shilling from every pound of the smack's earnings. This enabled a smart man to averge about five pounds a week, and should he ever be long enough ashore to enjoy it, to maintain a respectable and respected life-style. Traditions of payment differed, but usually the rest of the six or seven-man crew could augment their basic weekly wage, down to the boy-cook's one penny in the pound, earned from the profits of the voyage, so that all had a financial interest in its success. Merchant captains alone of the crew could rely upon a modest gratuity from the shipper to supplement their wage, and it was not unusual for them to hold shares in the vessel they commanded.

While the seasonal pattern of the fishing industry inevitably made for fluctuations, this was to some extent overcome by the introduction of convertor smacks (see section five) which were used for both trawling and driftnet fishing. Nevertheless the scale of the autumn herring fishing had traditionally attracted a motley crowd of casual workers seeking employment after the farmers' harvest was over, as well as individuals from inland villages who sought an alternative to the monotony of life on the land. A boat bound on a herring voyage, before the introduction of the steam capstan for hauling nets, required a complement of ten or eleven, and later semi-skilled hands were still recruited to clear the nets of fish at sea. Younger longshore fishermen supplemented their income by serving aboard seagoing drifters when the family-owned boat could no longer support them with its meagre earnings.

The smacksmen of the Essex rivers, particularly those of Rowhedge, Brightlingsea and Tollesbury, also with skipper-owned and family owned smacks, regularly fitted in service as professional crews aboard yachts during the summer, between fishing seasons. These were movements of individuals, unlike those which involved whole families that could occur when, due to the failure of the traditional fishery or to the attractions of a new one, groups moved together with their boats. A proportion of the Sheringham men moved north to Grimsby, south to Felixstowe and across the Thames estuary to Whitstable, where their distinctive boats were instantly recognisable.

Merchant seamen under sail served beneath a wider sky and a different tradition, although theirs was a slowly contracting world; steam beckoned the ambitious, while owners driven to reduce working expenses to the minimum cut down the number of the crew to the limits of safety. It was customary along the

East Coast for the crew to assist in trimming the cargo as it was loaded, to work the cargo winch when it was discharged, and then if necessary to clean out the hold. The oft-quoted remark that the crews "went to sea for the grub and earned their money working out the cargo" all too accurately describes the life.

By the turn of the century, the special skills required for sail repairs and renewing ropework aloft had become restricted to the mate, whose duties also included supervising the loading and stowing of the cargo. Work on the cargo winch was reserved for the seamen. It began at seven in the morning and continued until six in the evening. It must, however, be said that the gruelling work was traditionally preceded by a bacon and suet-duff breakfast, a rarity at sea, and as the cargo was frequently discharged into horse-drawn tumbrils at a rural quay, the operation was moderately paced. Unlike the smacks, where the skilled teamwork required for shooting and recovering the trawl could only be learnt through a long apprenticeship, it is hardly surprising that the crew contained a high proportion of drifters, unqualified in any particular trade. But these unfortunates were usually reinforced by one or two older seamen whose

The crews of Goldsmith's barges photographed in 1913 aboard the *Castanet* in Ipswich Dock with the firm's agent. Astern is the *Briton* and alongside is the *Thetis*.   *Roger Finch*

Sailing barges and Norfolk wherries at Yarmouth between the two world wars. The barge at left is the *Lady Jean*, one of the last wooden spritsail barges built; she was launched at Rochester in 1923.   *A. Pyner*

hard-won knowledge belonged to an age that had almost passed and for which they were unlikely to find a market elsewhere. They were veterans who once sailed aboard the crack brigantines and schooners that carried barrelled herrings to the Baltic and the Italian ports, returning with salt from Portugal, or had served in the Yarmouth barques regularly rounding Cape Horn in the copper ore trade.

Owners in the last days of sail could be grouped into three categories. Some vessels perpetuated the older tradition by being owned by up to five or six individuals who would spread their risk by taking up shares in a number of vessels. To judge from old registers, the owners displayed a considerable loyalty, and shares only rarely changed hands. One of the group might undertake the management of the vessel, while others, in their capacity of sailmaker, shipbuilder or ship chandler, would expect their interests to be studied when the ship was serviced. Smaller vessels tended to be owned by a trio, of whom one was the skipper, who secured cargoes and acted as his own book-keeper, along with two other members of his family. The success of the enterprise was dependent, like that of any small family business ashore, upon hard work and stringent economy. The remainder were wholly or part owned and managed as the extension of a shore-based enterprise which required the regular delivery of a raw material for its business. A coal merchant would have two or three boomie barges, or a miller a schooner upon which he knew he could rely to deliver flour uncontaminated by salt water, an arrangement which also enabled the vessel to temporarily "warehouse" consignments afloat when storage ashore was at a premium.

Of course these varying forms of ownership could overlap and change during a vessel's lifetime. Shipbuilders like Bayley of Ipswich would sometimes launch a vessel and run it as a speculation before either selling it outright or disposing of some shares in it. But whatever form of ownership existed, insurance against damage or disaster was essential to successful trading.

Although Harwich dropped out of the list of owners early on, its mutual insurance association for sailing craft owners lasted longer than those elsewhere. These associations had once existed at most ports, but due to its longevity, the Harwich Barge Alliance Insurance Association had on its list many of the last of the East Coast sailing craft. A mutual insurance association had, apart from the payment of a secretary and surveyor, no running expenses. Each member's

These barges alongside the quay at Mistley, the *Xylonite* and *Reliance*, were both owned by F. W. Horlock. The steel barge *Xylonite* was another of the last spritsail barges built, having been launched at Mistley in 1926. *Hervey Benham*

With lowered topsail and shortened mainsail, R. & W. Paul's *Anglia* scurries up the Thames to load one of the last commercial cargoes to be carried by an Ipswich-owned sailorman. Built at Ipswich in 1896, she was sold and converted to a barge yacht in 1961.
Roger Finch

vessel was valued and surveyed and then after an initial entrance fee of two or three per cent had been paid, the only other cost was the expense when a "call" was made. This was a levy, its amount relating to the value of a fellow member's vessel when it was lost or incurred damage. There were of course disadvantages to such a method of insurance. For instance a spell of exceptionally bad weather, covering an area where all the members traded, could bring down several calls upon members at a time when they themselves were showing little profit. But the numerous advantages outweighed them. It was profitable for members to assist fellow-subscribers in distress, without making salvage claims. A strong element of self-regulation was built into the system, for it was in the interest of all to see that bad seamanship was not tolerated and that inadequately manned vessels and poorly fitted out barges did not go to sea. The "mutual" also laid down what times of the year and where a vessel could trade and still rely on their cover. The flag of the "mutual" was flown by a vessel at sea in need of help so that other members of the association could come to its assistance. But it was also flown with a certain pride in port and appears in many of the traditional paintings of the sailing coasters and deep-sea traders.

The attraction of the London docks for bulk carriers, both sail and steam, was to some extent reversed by the improvement of the large East Coast ports in the latter half of the nineteenth century. Boston and King's Lynn both built coal-drops at which sailing coasters loaded Midland coal brought by rail. Ipswich improved its port facilities out of all recognition, which together with the introduction of steam towage enabled ocean-going sailing vessels carrying as much as five thousand tons of grain to discharge there. Much of this was either lightered, or distributed, by sailing barges to the Ipswich mills and depots as far afield as King's Lynn and Faversham.

Most of the waterside industries and the local gasworks required coal delivered by sea. As the older generation of ocean traders were forced back to coasting and coal work, it was found that the relatively big crews demanded to work their square canvas made slim profits even smaller. An answer to this was found by producing a bigger version of the traditional hard-chined barge hull, fitting it out with a ketch or schooner rig and so providing a cheap seagoing vessel with low overheads. This development took place in the fifties and sixties of the nineteenth century, particularly at Harwich, and the boomie or ketch barge proved to be economical to maintain and build. Those which were intended to fill the gap left by the fleet of deteriorating brigs and brigantines, or to replace them, carried some two hundred tons of coal and proved themselves to be a profitable compromise between inexpensive bulk cargo carriers and weatherly, sea-kindly sailing vessels. Like the barges they grew up from, they carried leeboards and were built with large hatches to facilitate loading and discharging.

The ketch barge *Pearl*, seen in a painting by Reuben Chappel. Built at Ipswich in 1889, she ended her days as a powder hulk on the Thames after a trading career of half a century.   *Private collection*

Smaller versions, some loading less than the coasting spritsail barges that followed them, managed summertime cargoes of coal from the Tyne, but were more at home loaded with the traditional East Anglian cargoes of malt, home-grown wheat and hardwood logs. They brought in "Guernsey fruit", as the stone chippings used for the roads were known, cattle food and timber. A few, like the little square-riggers before them, made epic voyages to Norway and Spain, but for the rest they were built to be servants to trades which made a voyage to Scotland an adventure and a cargo of grindstones from the Tyne to Rouen a break in a routine pattern of coasting work.

The ketch barges were in their turn replaced on the one hand by the motor coaster, capable of providing the reliability of a powered vessel while incurring the minimum of overhead expenses, and on the other by a new generation of powerful spritsail barges. Perhaps the general adoption of flexible steel wire rigging by the last decades of the nineteenth century had encouraged barge builders to rig a sailing vessel loading almost two hundred tons with the spritsail rig, which had earlier been considered only suitable for limited work at sea. Some of the big coasting barges combined the boomie barge's gaff mizzen and the sprit mainsail; known as mulies, they had higher rails than the conventional sprittie, heavy hatch coamings and sometimes, like the boomies, a wheelhouse.

To the mulies and the larger conventionally rigged spritsail barges went the distinction of being the last vessels dependent on sail alone to trade on the East Coast. For a decade after the end of the Second World War, coal came to Harwich and the Colne by sail, as it had done for centuries. Grain from London was delivered at Ipswich and Yarmouth and fertiliser from the Thames to King's Lynn. Beccles, Wells and Wisbech saw barges arrive, although no cargo-carrying sprittie visited Snape or Woodbridge after the end of the war. Ipswich saw as many as a dozen sailormen enter the dock on one tide; but eventually the end came, hastened by the demise of the London docks. In 1970, the mulie *Cambria* made her last voyage as a commercial trading vessel from Ipswich, and the days of East Coast sail were over.

Opposite top: Reuben Webb repairing a rudder on Pin Mill hard for the sailing barge *George Smeed* in 1949.   *Roger Finch*

Opposite bottom: A barge on the blocks for a refit and a new plank in the bottom.
          Roger Finch

Fishermen and Fishing Ways 3

THE FISHERIES of the East Coast from the Wash to the Thames Estuary provide a picture of remarkable richness and diversity.

Almost every town and village cherished its own traditions and produced its own type of craft, evolved and adapted to suit its own local conditions, ranging from the open boats working off the Norfolk and Suffolk beaches to the decked smacks and bawleys of the Essex estuaries. Some found their livelihood in the tide-tortured tumble of the North Sea and ventured as far afield as Iceland and the Solway Firth, others led a quieter though not necessarily less laborious life in their own creeks and estuaries or along their own foreshores.

Trawls and dredges, hand lines and long lines, drift nets and pots were among the techniques employed, and although most places regarded one of these as its speciality, fisheries were in the main so seasonal that most fishermen had to acquire a variety of skills and gear.

Up to the early years of the present century, freighting and fishing were still not wholly separate trades, with many a smack laying her fishing gear ashore to import a cargo of ponies and lobsters from Norway or potatoes from the Channel Islands, to use her speed to bring salmon from Scotland or fish from the North Sea fleets into Billingsgate, or to slog away down to the Tyne or the Humber for a few tons of coal. Smuggling, a useful sideline throughout the eighteenth century, was largely replaced in the nineteenth century by "salvaging"—the saving of wrecked ships, or if that was impossible, of their gear and cargo, and of lives before lifeboats were deemed a practical possibility. Some fishing craft were fitted out only for certain seasons; while they were laid up their crews went ashore to work on farms or in the brick fields or, especially in the nineteenth and early twentieth century in Essex, adopted a very different way of life as skippers and crews on yachts. This diversified pattern varied from century to century, indeed from generation to generation, largely in response to changing market demands and opportunities, among which the arrival of rail transport was the most important.

Amid all this kaleidoscopic diversity, three fisheries were of outstanding importance—oysters, cod and herrings. The two former, exceptionally, pro-

Reefed down in a strong breeze, Mersea oyster smacks set off for a day's work in the Blackwater. *Douglas Went*

Blakeney harbour at low water some years before the First World War. The schooner *Minstrel*, built at Wells in 1847, has arrived with coal while scallop fishing has brought in a Colchester-registered smack.   *Roger Finch*

vided a living not only all the year round, but throughout many centuries. The third was also ancient, but as far as the East Coast was concerned was essentially seasonal. In this brief account, these three "great" fisheries are first considered, followed by a survey of the coast from Norfolk to Essex.

The greatest oyster centres were in Essex, in the Colne, Blackwater, Crouch and Roach, and to a lesser extent at Leigh and across the estuary in Kent, but there were also fisheries along the whole length of the East Coast.

At King's Lynn both oyster and mussel beds, or scaups, as they were known, were officially protected in the sixteenth century, and in 1770 Lynn oysters, "the size of a horse's hoof", were popular at Stourbridge Fair. In 1875 there were seven principal beds employing seventy-nine boats from March to June. For fattening, the oysters were re-laid at Cleethorpes and in Heacham Harbour, on the North Norfolk coast. The fishery seems to have gone into a decline soon after this date.

Oysters were also abundant on the Burnham Flats and also between that harbour and Wells up to the mid-nineteenth century, but during the next thirty years were largely fished out by marauding Colchester smacks, though a little dredging continued until after the First World War. Boats from Stiffkey worked on the Dudgeon banks, leaving in the morning to dredge for a day and a night

36

and return on the morrow. Old oyster pits at Overy Staithe show that the trade was known there.

In the Alde, where old oyster pits may still be detected close to Orford quay, there was a fishery controlled by the Borough of Orford. This was several times piratically raided by Brightlingsea smacks in the seventeen-nineties. The Orwell fishery below Pin Mill also worked until after the First World War, was at one time big enough to achieve a European reputation and in the past had been used as a form of outdoor relief for the poor and aged seamen of Ipswich. There was another fishery in Harwich harbour, raided by the Brightlingsea men in 1774. The Deben also received the attention of the Colchester men, and there were oysters to be found in the Walton Backwaters.

In the nineteenth century heyday, the industry ranged from the proud and ancient concerns at Colchester and Whitstable down to hundreds of little private layings in every creek and estuary. Most dredgermen laboured quietly in their home waters, using little ten-ton cutter-rigged smacks or double-ended "haul-tow" skiffs with which dredges were hauled up and down the creek layings

Essex oyster smacks.

between anchors. But the bigger smacks ranged far afield—down the East Coast as far as the Firth of Forth, down Channel to Falmouth, and then "round the land" to Mumbles in Wales (where the local fishermen so admired them that they built copies for their own use) and even to the Solway. In most of these places the Essex men were cordially and justifiably detested as marauders and pillagers.

A fleet of sixty Essex smacks braved the hazards of capture by the French during the Napoleonic wars to sail down Channel each spring to dredge rich grounds off Jersey, and they continued to do so till the grounds were exhausted by 1871. Dredging in French territorial waters prolonged international friction after the restoration of peace, culminating in the seizure of the *Hebe* of Brightlingsea by a French gunboat in 1832.

The other major foreign oyster fishery was off Terschelling on the Dutch coast. Working on what was usually the lee side of the North Sea, among treacherous sands, with no harbour of refuge available, this was a particularly cruel trade. Finally Brightlingsea lost five smacks and over thirty men in the winter gales of 1883, after which even the Colne "skillingers" were discouraged.

The annual cod voyage "Icelandward by the Grace of God" is the most ancient and romantic of all the East Coast fishing traditions. It was carried on from Dunwich in the early Middle Ages, King's Lynn and Cromer in the fourteenth century, and from most of the ports between Boston and London, with particular emphasis on Southwold, in Tudor times. The fishing was with hand lines, two hooks to a line, and so it continued from Harwich, and surprisingly Aldeburgh, into the early years of the twentieth century.

Three distinct seasons were observed. The twenty-two-week Iceland voyage commenced at Easter; then in the autumn the smacks fitted out for long-lining on the coast, laying lines from the smack but hauling them from the smack's boat

Opposite: Herring drifters, part clinker and part carvel planked, hauled out on a Yarmouth shipyard in the eighteen-eighties. In the foreground is a horse capstan used for hauling out.
Robert Malster

Right: "Half and halfers", as the smaller herring luggers were known at Southwold, lying at Walberswick quay in the eighteen-seventies.
Suffolk Photographic Survey

in the strong tides; when spring came, they went long-lining on the Dogger, working with the lines entirely from the smacks. Boats fitted with wet-wells which had not gone to Iceland often made summer voyages to Norway for cargoes of lobsters, which, like the cod, were stored in floating fish chests in Harwich harbour, waiting the demands of the London market.

As the demand for fresh-killed cod increased at Billingsgate, so Barking, Gravesend and Greenwich developed in importance, since cod could be sailed to market in a tide. Then in the mid-nineteenth century the opening of the railway to Grimsby reversed the trend, for the smacks could be based on the Humber, nearer the Dogger grounds, and still meet the London demand for fish by rail. The rapid growth in the eighteen-sixties of Grimsby sucked much of the life out of most of the fishing ports on the East Coast, particularly those which depended on the trawling industry, and indeed down Channel as far as the West Country. The Manningtree smacks were the pioneer settlers in the headlong conversion of a sleepy Lincolnshire village into the greatest fishing centre in the world. Among those who followed were many from Greenwich and Harwich. The leading Barking firm, Hewett's, made its exodus no further than Gorleston at the entrance to the Yare, where in the eighteen-sixties it played a leading part in the change from long-lining to trawling.

The most famous of all the East Coast callings was however the herring fishery. Dating back as far as the cod fishery, it attained an even greater importance and a much greater recognition, for it continued to increase up to the First World War and lasted into the nineteen-fifties.

Up to the mid-eighteenth century this, the greatest harvest of the North Sea, was dominated by the Dutch. Government efforts to compete included in 1753 the Society of the Free British Fishery, with a fleet of busses at Southwold (still

Lowestoft trawling smacks leaving harbour in the early years of the present century and, opposite, the Lowestoft drifter *Dawn of Day*, in a painting by George Vemply Burwood dated 1895.   *Roger Finch*

recalled by the name Buss Creek), but it was not till the early nineteenth century that a viable English fishery became established at Yarmouth with the unhandy square-rigged busses evolving into three-masted luggers. Lowestoft, where there had long been a vigorous fishery off the beach, became a rival with the building of a harbour and later a railway, and for a century the two centres developed their own ever-increasing fleets, with the luggers giving way to dandies and ketches and the hybrid convertor smacks, and then to steam drifters. Both centres served as host to the Scottish fishermen and curers who followed the herring down the coast, till in 1913, the record year, there were 406 boats fishing out of Yarmouth (264 local, 142 Scottish) and 770 out of Lowestoft (350 local, 420 Scottish), with an overflow at Southwold. In addition to the deep-sea drifters an inshore herring fishery has been carried on for centuries, with small open or half-decked boats known as punts, sometimes working out of the major ports, but usually off the beaches of Norfolk and Suffolk.

The herring fishery did not traditionally extend to Essex, though at West Mersea long cotton drift nets, 200 yards in one piece, were formerly employed. Such unusual gear suggests a tradition of some long standing, but by 1939 it was almost forgotten, though a dredgerman would sometimes pass an evening low water drifting a piece of old thirty-three-yard Yarmouth or Lowestoft net with his smack's boat in Salcot creek. The fish caught were the locally spawned estuary herrings, a species inferior to the North Sea herring, and the lack of a market was the reason they were not taken more seriously. This market was provided by the collapse of the North Sea fishery in the nineteen-fifties and since then a score or so of boats have found a living throughout the winter.

If oysters, cod and herrings represent the great classic fisheries of the East Coast, others were even more important to certain places at certain periods. Fish trawling has been carried on almost everywhere for centuries as soles, plaice, roker and dabs made their seasonal appearances along the coast. Traditionally it was more important in Essex than on the Suffolk and Norfolk shores, for the Essex cutter was more suited to tow a beam trawl than were the luggers off the East Anglian beaches.

A brief survey of the coast from Norfolk to Essex will give some idea of the diversity of craft and the trades they pursued—inevitably with many omissions, for every place had its own local traditions, and the whole picture of the East Coast fisheries in the age of sail would fill a larger book than this.

That strange corner of the North Sea, the Wash, is, when the tide floods, a wide and wild expanse of open water; when the tide ebbs it is a maze of deep and changing channels running between huge tracts of sand and mud. It has few

fish, but the channels remain the home of the one surviving pink shrimp fishery in Britain, and the shoals are one of the country's richest sources of mussels and cockles.

These waters have from time immemorial been shared, with more acrimony than harmony, by Boston and its Lincolnshire outports and King's Lynn and its Norfolk associates. Down the centuries the balance of importance in the inshore fisheries has swung between the two sides of the Wash, though Lynn never developed anything to compare with Boston's two nineteenth-century trawling companies, which at the turn of the century between them owned thirty-seven deep-sea steam trawlers.

The mussel fishery has for centuries been the most important trade in the Wash, along with cockling. In the days of sail, these shellfish were gathered by hand by men working on the sands and mudbanks, the boats being used only for transport. Some of the longshore scaups were worked direct into carts, dispensing with boats altogether.

Lynn Corporation received powers over its local waters under a charter of Henry VIII and in 1560 four persons were appointed "as in times past" to go with the fishermen to the scaups "to see peace kept". But it was not until the eighteen-seventies that Boston and Lynn were given full powers of control over their oyster and mussel fisheries, starting an energetic system of regulation and development operated since 1897 by the Eastern Sea Fisheries Joint Committee, with its launch *Protector* and bailiffs (some part-time) at all the ports.

Lays, or "marine allotments", were licensed at first on a basis of one acre per

Opposite: The King's Lynn fleet coming out of the Fisher Fleet and driving down the Ouse towards the Wash.

Right: The long lean hull of the Lynn shrimper is clearly seen in this photograph taken at the entrance to the Fisher Fleet.

person at Lynn and five acres at Boston, with sixty acres on the Thief Sand granted to a fishermen's association. Mussels were transplanted from one scaup to another, sometimes in quantities of over 300 tons. These scaups, which were mudbanks, sometimes created or developed by the mussels themselves, numbered seventeen at Lynn in 1875, the largest, the Lower Daisley, being a mile long and averaging 300 yards in breadth. Thousands of hazel stakes were driven in the scaups as spat collectors, sometimes with collars on them to discourage crabs from climbing them.

The craft employed in these fisheries, and in the oyster fishery already mentioned, are described in Section five (The Wash smack and The Lynn shrimper). There were, however, some other occupations.

Stowboating for sprats was carried out on ebb tides in Boston Deeps and Lynn Well up to the First World War, but the short thirty-six-foot nets did not compare in size with their Essex equivalents and the trade was entirely for manure. The Essex men's hip ropes or templines were called weagles, but details and names of the rest of the gear seem forgotten.

In 1900 six Boston boats and one or two from Lynn were employed. There was also a form of stow-net known as a trim, which had a triangular mouth, about sixteen feet along each of its three sides, with a net about sixteen yards long to the cod end or "swinge". The tiny mesh net was criticised for the destruction of much immature stock, as it was in the case of shrimp trawls.

Herring drift nets were not suitable for the difficult Wash channels, and instead nets were staked out on the mussel scaups. Staked nets, up to three-quarters of a mile in length, were also set for flounders, here known as butts, which were also foul-hooked by towing an iron bar armed with hooks, known as a "murderer". In season, smelt were taken in ring-net seines above the bridge at Fosdyke, and in trim nets in places including the Ouse below Denver Sluice. Shrimping was usually brought to an end by the first frosts, and shellfish did not support all the men through the winter. Some took jobs in seagoing ships; others made what they could from wildfowling. Seals' noses also fetched a ten-shilling reward from the Eastern Sea Fisheries Committee.

The shellfish trade extended along the North Norfolk coast. The rights from Thornham Harbour to Wolferton Creek have been vested, for at least nine centuries, with the Le Strange family, a reward according to legend for mobilising the villagers of the Wash against Danish invaders, conferred along with the title Lord High Admiral of the Wash.

In modern times the family sought to provide relief for the poor around Hunstanton by allowing them to gather shellfish, but with the general depression of the nineteen-thirties even this modest activity ceased, and in 1935 the maritime estate was leased to William Loose, a Brancaster fisherman whose grandson, John Henry Loose, works it today. As a result Brancaster Staithe,

The Lynn shrimper *Rob-Pete* and other craft in the Fisher Fleet at King's Lynn, with a cockle boat in the foreground. *Robert Malster*

A flatbottom or canoe used in North Norfolk for mussel gathering.
Robert Malster

which has the additional advantage of a clean tidal harbour, fed by calcium-bearing freshwater streams which encourage shell growth, remains the chief survivor among the North Norfolk ports, most of which have seen their fisheries die out.

The mussel lays were kept clean of pests and when their contents were sold out at the end of the winter they were dug over to give a hard base. Then in spring they were re-stocked from the old Le Strange scaups or from the Wash. In the days of sail this involved a difficult voyage for a small boat with a perishable cargo at a season all too prone to easterly winds. As one man put it "It's O.K. for the Brancaster men because they've only got to come around Holland Point through Brancaster Bay and into the harbour. That's enough. Wells is a little more than enough, but if you have to come to Blakeney, well, sometimes you just could not make it."

Methods have changed but little. Musselling is still a manual operation, in contrast to the mechanisation of the bigger Dutch grounds. Up to two tons a day are gathered, mostly by hand rake into a net for transfer by row boat to the smack. Tractors to a limited extent continue the horse and cart tradition, but, apart from the aversion of machinery for salt water, boats are still the most efficient transport.

Mussels grow best between the low water marks of spring and neap tides. Thus on a spring ebb they are exposed and can be lifted with a fork, being so matted together that they do not fall between the prongs, but on neap tides they often have to be reached under water. For this a special type of rake was used. Called a "dydle rake" at Brancaster, a "wim" at Stiffkey and a "lab rake" at Wells, it comprised a bar with about seven teeth and a net behind it, fixed to a whippy handle of larch or ash up to eighteen feet long.

To ferry the mussels from the scaups to the fishing boats, home-made punts known as canoes were used. Around sixteen feet long, they were built of three or

45

Sheringham fishermen preparing to set off after crabs. The lines of a typical North Norfolk crab boat are well seen on the opposite page; the design has been adapted but not greatly altered since the coming of motors. *Robert Malster*

four one-and-a-half-inch planks to give a four-foot wide bottom and a vestigial transom stern. Before the sides were put on, a wedge was driven under one end of the bottom to bring it up an inch or two; a perfectly flat-bottomed canoe would suck down in the mud when loaded and fail to float. They were called canoes at Blakeney but flatbottoms at Wells—the alternative name never being used in the other place.

Both mussel scaups and cockle grounds were liable to sudden disaster and ultimate recovery, with the result that periods of glut were often succeeded by shortages so severe that areas with immature stocks had to be closed to fishing. As well as mussels the cockle trade was also taken seriously at Brancaster. Cockles were not relaid in the harbour on lays, but the sandy sides of the channel were dug level and the banks strengthened to give them an even tidal flow, free of turbulence. Despite these efforts, driving sand covered the banks and the havoc to the cockles was completed by oyster-catchers after the establishment of a nearby bird sanctuary in 1924.

After the oysters failed, whelking occupied twelve boats at Brancaster fifty years ago, but with the Wash and Brancaster Bay now largely cleared of whelks only three survive. Some alternative occupations were also open to the Norfolk shell fisherman. From April to August nets were set from thirty to a hundred and fifty yards off the shore for sea trout, and a less spectacular but more reliable alternative was to stop the creek and beat the water to drive everything from butts to mullet into the net.

The story of Brancaster could be repeated at most of its neighbouring ports with some variations.

Wells, where a fleet of thirty-two fishing boats in 1844 had declined thirty years later to a couple of lining cobles, saw the start of a revival in the eighteen-nineties, when whelking spread there from overcrowded Sheringham. At first little lug-rigged twenty-two-foot hubblers were used, their forward orruck holes stuffed with sacking, but the twenty-mile sea voyage called for decked boats, which were used at Brancaster. Today's Wells whelkers favour ex-R.N.L.I. lifeboats, good at sea, though less handy for pot-hauling than a purpose-built fishing boat.

Though the Wells mussel lays were in 1875 said to have been wasted away, in 1909 fifty-five lays were worked by twenty-five licensees, and though these in their turn have vanished the port has remained active with skate, taken by lining cobles a century ago but now trawled, sprats, now taken by mid-water trawls, and other fishing in season. At Blakeney, thirty men had lays in the harbour and in Cley Channel in 1909, but there is only a flicker of activity here and at Overy Staithe today.

Stiffkey was noted for cockles—the famous "Stewkey Blues", which were

Beach boats in Norfolk and Suffolk: above are double-ended fishing boats on Caister beach and on the opposite page Southwold fishermen clean their nets after a spratting trip. Although most Suffolk beach boats have a transom, the nearest boat is double ended like those north of Yarmouth. *Robert Malster*

cultivated in lays and worked by "poor women", to the number of a hundred in 1875, and twenty to thirty in 1909. These women used a knife bent at right angles to its handle to skim off the top half-inch of soil and reveal the cockles. Once one or two were scratched out, their nimble fingers would flick them into the palms of their hands and thence into the nets, sorting the large ones in the process.

All along this coast the crabbers worked off the beaches. While they took their name from their principal trade, which they carried out from March to October, they also drifted for herrings in spring and autumn, for mackerel in summer and for sprats in winter, when they also went long-lining for cod, roker and plaice. Fish trawling was tried only when the crabbing was very slack, but a few trawled for shrimps.

In addition to the two classes of beach boat described in Section five the Sheringham and Cromer men joined in the deep-sea fishing with their so-called "great boats". These were in fact two-masted luggers, which fitted out in spring for crabbing off the Yorkshire coast, working their pots with a capstan, followed by autumn mackerel and herring drifting and winter cod-lining. With crews of a dozen, they were too big for beaching and when they did occasionally visit their home ports the catches had to be ferried ashore. Their winter lay-up was at

Morston Creek or Yarmouth. Their crews were employed on a share basis by businessmen and possibly philanthropists who seem to have established the "great boats" early in the nineteenth century. The fleet numbered about forty in the 1860s, mostly owned in Sheringham, but disappeared under the competition of the steam drifter at the turn of the century. Around 1870 the main dipping lug was replaced by a gaff mainsail, following the example of the Yarmouth and Lowestoft herring "luggers".

Crabs and lobsters were originally taken in hoop nets which were set singly and picked up after an hour or two, but in the eighteen-sixties pots were introduced. At first they were used singly, like hoops, but soon they came to be joined in shanks, of about twenty-five pots (thirty-six at Brancaster), with a three-man boat working about seven shanks and a two-man boat about six. Pots could be set in shanks and left overnight, a system so much more productive that it was soon blamed for any periodical shortages. The price was of course the risk of losing gear when bad weather blew up, but it was worth paying. Hoops, however, continued to find favour for a specific lobster fishery which employed thirty men at Sheringham in the early spring before the First World War, and as we shall see they were used at Harwich till the end of the lobster fishery there.

Beach boats were to be found along the Norfolk and Suffolk coast as far south as Bawdsey, just north of the Deben. South of Happisburgh they were often designated "punts", and were usually dragged up the beaches on "skeets"

rather than carried, and so could be larger than the double-ended crabbers and dispense with their "orrucks". In Norfolk, they ranged from eighteen feet to twenty-five feet, and were double ended, the largest setting a standing lug mizzen as well as a dipping lug foresail. At Aldeburgh they were from fifteen to twenty feet, with a short iron bumkin for the tack of the dipping lug. Here winter sprat-drifting, using nets with a smaller mesh than for herrings, was again added to the usual alternation of spring and autumn herring drifting, summer potting and winter lining. Fish trawling in summer was also sufficiently important to justify rigging a gaff mainsail in some of the boats.

Surprisingly, open boats were not confined to the beaches but were favoured even where there were harbours. The "punts" at Yarmouth were up to thirty-seven feet long, and at Lowestoft up to thirty-five feet, clinker-built and rigged with two lugs. It was claimed they could be worked with two fewer men than a decked boat would require. Decked cutters and dandies, up to forty feet long, known as "wolders", were, however, also used at Yarmouth and Lowestoft to trawl the channel inside the Haisborough Sand, the Wold.

The extent to which beach boats built in the style of the North Country coble were used is a mystery. E. W. Cooke included an engraving of a Yarmouth coble in his classic *Shipping and Craft* (1829), they appear in paintings, and half-models have been found in Ipswich and elsewhere. This suggests they were used to some extent on the Norfolk and Lincolnshire coast—a reminder of the dangers of accepting any tidy classification of local craft.

When one reaches the Orwell, the scene changes from open shores facing the North Sea to creeks and estuaries giving on to the labyrinthine sands of the Thames Estuary. Instead of clinker-built open boats, we now find decked smacks and bawleys, adapted for different fishing techniques, though by the time we reach the end of the survey at Leigh the comparisons are again with the place where we started, the Wash.

The Harwich men never adopted pots, either for whelks or lobsters. For the former they preferred trot lines, carrying about two hundred snoods on which half a dozen crabs were speared, using a foot-long needle. The crabs were obtained in Handford Water and as far afield as Mersea and kept alive for weeks in tightly packed bags—a fishery to catch bait with which to catch bait! Trot lines had to be picked up gently, for which purpose a boat with a deep forefoot was favoured, so that it could be rowed steadily up the line, pulling on the lee oar. These fifteen foot whelk skiffs were specially built at Harwich for £6 each, rising later to one pound a foot.

The Harwich men also retained hoop nets for their lobstering, which employed up to thirty smacks and bawleys, including four from Manningtree and two from Aldeburgh, working on the West Rocks and the Roughs. The hoops were of thin upright section like a barrel hoop about eighteen inches across, and were called "edge-uppers". This shape could be lifted more quickly

The bawley *Ethel*, one of a number of first class bawleys built by Cann at Harwich.
Nautical Photo Agency

51

than a hoop of a round section. Small fish were dried for bait, the best being "slips" (small soles) which dried as hard as teak. The hoops were worked by boats towed out to the grounds by the bawleys. They had to be picked up at slack water, as the buoys did not "watch" when the tide ran hard, but were washed below the surface. The hoops were picked up with the tide, and the fisherman could feel at once if there was a lobster. These boats used eight hoops, but with the introduction of motor bawleys this increased to forty hoops, and inevitably the grounds were soon fished out.

Shrimping and cockling were two fisheries common both to the Wash and the Thames Estuary and worked on broadly similar lines.

While the Thames Estuary shrimp fishery belonged traditionally to Leigh and Gravesend, the centre of activity largely shifted to Harwich after rail transport enabled shrimps to be sent to London from a port close to the fishing grounds in the Wallet and the adjacent outer estuary channels, which were less affected by industrial pollution than those grounds further up the Thames.

A Leigh bawley, with a shrimp trawl aboard, in light airs.
Hervey Benham

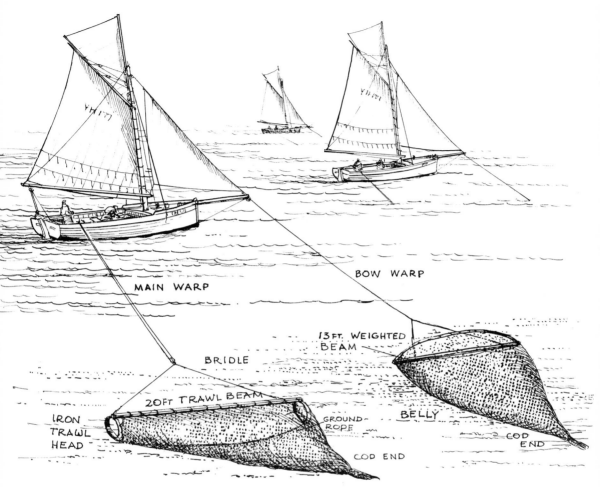

MAIN WARP

BOW WARP

13 FT. WEIGHTED BEAM

BRIDLE

20 FT TRAWL BEAM

BELLY

IRON TRAWL HEAD

GROUND-ROPE

COD END

COD END

Shrimp trawls in use.

The traditional shrimp trawl had a scraper board on the ground (like an oyster dredge) with the net supported above it—perhaps a survival of the medieval version of the fish trawl. At Leigh and Gravesend (where the gear was known as a "trim-tram" or "sluke and ledge" gear) the net was supported by a prop, the "right-up stick", set in the middle of the ground scraper, with a triangular wooden extension ahead of the scraper to which the tow warp was attached. The Yarmouth shrimpers raised their net in a curve or bow, with one or more uprights, for which reason it was called a "bow" net. They used a rope bridle instead of the wooden "sluke". Rather than increase the size of these trawls, several small ones were used, a practice continued when a beam above the net, raised on iron heads, came to replace the scraper board. The Leigh men were specially fond of booming out their small trawls to keep them clear of each other and to cover as much ground as possible. A Yarmouth shrimper sometimes chose to shoot one beam trawl and two "bow" nets. The Wash system of hauling two trawls is described in Section five (The Lynn shrimper). At Harwich between the wars single trawls with beams around twenty-six feet long had come into general favour.

Up to the end of the nineteenth century shrimps were brought ashore to be cooked everywhere they were caught. There was a boiler for the purpose in the Harwich Navy Yard. Even though they were kept in wells, this left the catch flabby and tasteless, without the crisp texture and pink colour that are the secrets of their appeal. A Leighman (it is claimed) introduced the practice of cooking them aboard, and soon all the bawleys were fitted with boilers, from which they probably took their name. Bawleys from Leigh and smacks from Tollesbury and Wivenhoe joined the local fleet at Harwich, and up to eighty shrimpers would sail on the tide.

This trade did not end, as so many did, through over-fishing or a market failure but through the disappearance of the sandy growth known as "ross" on

A stowboat net.

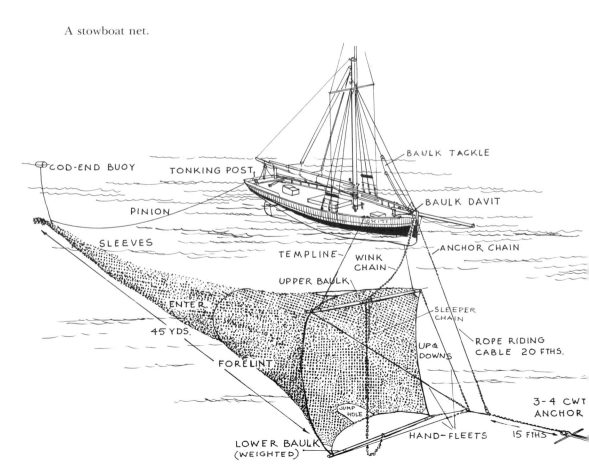

which the shrimps fed. An armed lead or a moused dredge was employed to search for the "ross", and as soon as it was detected the shrimper shot his trawl.

The stowboat net, the great (in both senses) speciality of the Thames Estuary, was a huge fish trap of remarkable complexity and ingenuity, which almost seems to have anticipated in the Middle Ages the industrial fishing techniques of modern times. Certainly it attracted a comparable odium, for it was outlawed by Parliament in 1488, despite which it continued to be used for five centuries for taking the annual winter sprat harvest, till it finally became obsolete in the nineteen-fifties. The tapering net, 150 yards long, was slung below the anchored smack, its mouth extended by two twenty-foot baulks, twenty feet apart. These baulks were connected by "handfleets" to the anchor chain, and their depth was controlled by "templines" supporting the upper baulk below the smack. A "wind chain", worked by the windlass, closed and raised the baulks, and a rope from the distant cod end, the "pinion" was belayed to a "tonking post" on the smack's quarter. One might think it a half-day's work to set such a trap, yet the stowboat smacks, guided only by swooping seagulls, succeeded in anchoring down-tide of the shoals and getting the whole apparatus in the water in a matter of minutes, always in tricky tidal waters and the worst weather of the year.

Brightlingsea, Wivenhoe and Rowhedge were the traditional ports, but there were also stowboaters at Harwich, Aldeburgh and King's Lynn. During the second half of the nineteenth century Tollesbury adopted the trade, establishing one of the few successful fishermen's co-operatives, Tolfish Ltd, but still using Brightlingsea for landing. Throughout the first half of the twentieth century Brightlingsea was as much a sprat port in winter as Harwich was a shrimp town in summer, with hundreds of tons of sprats dumped for manure after the demands of Billingsgate and the local fish shops had been met.

Mackerel were formerly drift-netted from the Wash to West Mersea, using a larger mesh than that of the otherwise similar herring drift-net, but since the First World War they have become almost entirely a West Country speciality. Twenty boats were employed at Lowestoft in 1854, but only three in 1862. At Yarmouth the season lasted from 12th March to 12th July, but this fishery was in decline in the eighteen-seventies. Details of mackerel voyages from West Mersea in 1791 are contained in the surviving notebook of a fisherman, William Haward, whose catches amounted to the then not inconsiderable sum of £50 a voyage.

As for the tasty smelt, a once-prized catch in most tidal estuaries from the Welland to the Medway, he also is only a memory. Smelts were important in the Wash rivers and Breydon Water, where they were dragged ashore in eighty-yard seine nets so successfully that a close season was observed from April to August in the Eastern Sea Fisheries district. Their scarcity was blamed on the use of the destructive trim-nets.

There were other fisheries great and small, too numerous to describe in detail, employing open boats or half-deckers. Every tidal creek along the coast, along with the runnels and low-ways on such sands as the Maplins, has at some time been stopped by a peter net set across it to catch chiefly flounders and grey mullet as the tide ebbed. This, as the name suggests, was the staple trade of the Leigh peter boats, which preceded and developed into the larger bawleys. This method of stop-net fishing was the chief medieval method, using elaborate permanent fish traps known as weirs, kettles or kiddles. They were set up on every shoal and shallow, to the profit of the monasteries and manors, which often enjoyed a monopoly, and to the annoyance of trading vessels which found them an obstruction to navigation. The last evidence can still be seen at exceptionally low tides when the stumps of decayed posts are revealed.

Eeels were a seasonal interest all down the coast, with a variety of techniques employed. Tapering funnels of net, set on cane hoops, with lead-in nets to direct the eels into the first hoop, were known as "fyke nets". They were also set, without the lead-in nets, behind sluices at locks and water mills. Norfolk marshmen worked "setts" across the Broadland rivers. These comprised a net, corked and leaded, into which were worked several funnel pockets, known as "pods". The whole gear could be held down on the bottom of the river by day, to allow craft to pass over it, and allowed to surface at night. Catches of up to 100 stone were not unknown in a night's fishing. In Essex, at Manningtree, a sixty-yard seine net was used, with a pocket at the bunt, and eels were also trawled, "babbed" (caught by worms on woollen snoods, without hooks) and "sheared" (using trident-like metal spears) according to season. At West Mersea, in the times when all the creeks and shores grew rich carpets of "eel grass", a shorter seine was used. Only twenty yards long and three fathoms deep, with a

An Essex oyster smack on the hard at Tollesbury. *Robert Malster*

Stowboaters discharging their autumn catch of sprats at Brightlingsea in the nineteenth-twenties.   *Douglas Went*

pocket at one end, it was called an "eel bumper". The end with the pocket was fixed to a withy or stake driven in the mud close to the shore, and the net was rowed round in a circle. As it was picked up, the eels were shaken down into the pocket.

In the times when oysters spawned each spring, it was important to provide clean shell or "culch" for the spat to settle on. Much of this was found on "shram hills", one of which, on Mersea Nass, was so high and steep that boats could go alongside and be loaded without trouble. But good culch was also worth dredging and fetched a shilling a tub—especially "blue" culch from near the Nore in the Thames Estuary. The pitched battles between neighbouring oystermen common down the centuries were not confined to raids on layings, but extended to the protection of precious culch reserves. Tollesbury dredger-men forcibly boarded Burnham smacks dredging culch on the Bench Head in the Blackwater in 1893, an assault leading to the last charge of piracy in English

Oyster smacks setting off from Mersea for the day's work.   *Douglas Went*

legal history. Tiles and other forms of spat collectors have been tried in recent years, but the spatfalls have been so poor that they have achieved no great success.

Essex men have put the dredges to which they were so accustomed to other purposes besides oyster-catching. "Five-fingers" (starfish) fetched £1 a ton for fertiliser before the time of "artificials", and were taken on the Colne Bar and nearby Knoll Sand, as well as on the Kentish flats by Rowhedge smacks, using oyster dredges with the rigging slacked back to increase their capacity. Four men working sixteen dredges could load ten tons in a tide, but it was hectic work, for while the full dredge "swam" easily to the surface its contents then became a dead weight of a full hundredweight to heave aboard. Each man with his own four dredges to handle thus had to help his neighbour with the final heave, for it needed two men on the chapstick to tip the contents into the hold. The loading was so fast that each time a man could spare a moment to glance at a nearby smack he saw her lower in the water. The work was not over when the smacks returned, either to a Colchester hard, or in the case of Tollesbury smacks a farmer's dock, for the "fives" settled into a solid mass which had to be dug out with a fork. Once they were spread on the land they soon degenerated into a white powder. This trade finished by 1920. An attempt to revive it in the nineteen-fifties succeeded as far as the catching went, but the corrosive fluid draining from the "fives" which had not troubled wooden farm wagons was found so destructive to motor lorries that no-one would handle them.

Garfish (in Essex known as gorbills) were once important in the Blackwater, as medieval records of a garfish weir opposite Stansgate recall. Mersea men within living memory used a gorbill ring net, 150 fathoms long, two fathoms deep, corked and leaded, with a square hole in the middle having a "poke" or cod end laced in. This was set from a rowboat, the object being to complete the ring neatly. But as an insurance against error a fifty-yard "guess-line" was also carried, to be employed if the fisherman misjudged his circle. As the net was pulled in a man stirred the water over the boat's stern with an oar to scare the fish, for if one jumped the net all the rest followed. Perhaps the special garfish seine used during May at Wells in 1875 was something of this kind.

The humble winkle was picked up all along the coast, and particularly in the Wash, till the ground there was ruined by barnacles introduced, in the belief of the fishermen, on ships from the Southern Hemisphere. Mersea men were among the last to pursue it. Their smaller oyster smacks spent a week on "the Main"—the Dengie shore between Bradwell and the Crouch—lying in the Grange and Hoo outfalls, and sixty years ago as many as thirty Mersea men would be winkling on the mudflats beside the Harwich rivers. The little sailing bumkins popular in Mersea to this day are still affectionately known as "winkle brigs". It is said that while they lay under the universal carpet of eel grass (*Zostera*) the winkles were green and large, but when the grass vanished in the nineteen-twenties—the worst ecological disaster to befall the Essex creeks and estuaries—they turned small, black and barnacle-ridden. More important, the mud banks on which they lived began to wash away, a process of erosion still to be seen.

Local types of fishing craft, peculiar to different places and reflecting their needs and traditions, became less recognisable after the Second World War. A new generation of fishermen preferred stock steel or G.R.P. hulls, fitted with wheelhouses, winches and deck gear to their own taste, or bought craft from any country where they were available, particularly from Belgium and Holland, where overfishing had already put whole fleets out of business. Scottish, French and Dutch boats are now commoner in most East Coast fishing ports than the products of local yards.

Among the bigger boats, more powerful engines, with a voracious thirst for expensive diesel fuel, have permitted the use of ever heavier and more destructive trawls, while smaller boats have resorted to synthetic fibre gill nets, the lavish and often careless use of which has decimated many stocks. Electronic fish-finding and navigation equipment has come to be regarded as essential. As a result, higher costs have demanded bigger catches at a time when many once productive grounds are being fished out. The riches of the North Sea, which seemed inexhaustible, and which served for so many centuries, have largely succumbed to man's greed and his technical ingenuity.

The fisheries of the future will no doubt be largely regulated by rules and restrictions, quotas and licences, imposed by European as well as national and local decree. In the leisure age now struggling to be born the fishermen will probably include a high proportion of part-timers. Certainly the old communities, providing a way of life for succeeding generations, will not be seen again.

Indian Summer of the Workboats 4

WHEN in the nineteen-fifties the spritsail barge, last survivor among sailing traders, finally surrendered to the heavy motor lorry, and the new generation of inshore fishermen found more efficient alternatives to the smacks their grandfathers had built and their fathers had inherited, it looked as if traditional craft would vanish for ever from the face of the waters they had so long graced. In fact there was a remarkable revival, still continuing and at that time unforeseen and unimagined. Today, thirty years later, more than fifty sailing barges are in commission, a wherry again sails on the Norfolk Broads, a keel and sloop on the Humber, and well over forty smacks and bawleys cruise and race out of Essex and Kentish ports, with another ten still under reconstruction.

The new generation of amateur sailormen have their own Thames Barge Sailing Club, which first restored *Arrow* (now no more) and *Asphodel*, and which now owns *Pudge* and the Harwich-built *Centaur*, in which its members enjoy weekend and week-long cruises. The associated Society for Spritsail Barge Research specialises in the history of these craft, past and present. Attempts to maintain traditional craft in traditional trades have not succeeded. A brave endeavour to find such employment for the sprittie *Memory*, long owned at Ipswich, did not attract sufficient support from merchants, but out of this venture grew the East Coast Sail Trust, which chartered her for schools, later replacing her with *Thalatta*, supplemented for some years by the *Sir Alan Herbert* (ex *Lady Jean*, like the *Thalatta* owned for many years by R. & W. Paul), renamed after a distinguished lover of barges and patron of the Trust.

Of the many other barges now afloat, some like the *Ena* and *May* have been restored by companies to offer a novel form of hospitality and relaxation for customers and staff, or for advertising and sales promotion. Others have been the enterprise of individuals, following the example of the artist W. L. Wyllie, who converted the *New Zealand* and renamed her *Four Brothers* at the beginning of the century, and of Cyril Ionides' "floating home" (immortalised in his book of that name) which were among the first of all the yacht barges. But most of today's private owners find it necessary to meet some of the formidable upkeep and running costs by passenger chartering.

The little Maldon smack *Kate*, one of a number of oyster smacks which have been preserved by enthusiasts. *Robert Malster*

That so many hulls have been found fit to re-rig, or capable of being restored to that condition, and so much gear discovered or made anew to rig them, is remarkable. Fortunately many of the best had been converted into motor barges and so maintained in a seaworthy condition. Others, some once part of the Colchester-based fleet of Francis and Gilders Ltd, had been relegated to lightering timber into Heybridge Basin before the canal trade to Chelmsford ceased, and had the good fortune to be cared for there with such devotion that they escaped major deterioration.

The range of sailing barges that have survived as conversions extends from the great steel *Will*, ex *Will Everard*, one hundred and fifty registered tons and ninety-seven feet overall, to the diminutive *Cygnet*. The latter, only forty-one feet from stem to stern and of thirteen registered tons, was rebuilt at Pin Mill in 1986 exactly a century after her launch. She preserves the mizzen mounted on the rudder head, has tiller steering and a cabin top that extends from rail to rail, a unique survival and a quaint contrast to the spritties twice her length which can usually be seen under repair or renovation by Fred Webb close by.

Britain's oldest wooden vessel afloat, the smack *Boadicea*, built 1808, which has been rebuilt by her owner, Michael Frost.   *Roger Finch*

The Wash smack *Freda and Norah*, cut down to a motor fishing boat before her restoration to sail.   *Robert Malster*

By the sixties many young men were falling under the spell, and showing an ability in DIY shipwrighting hitherto unimagined. The example was largely set by Michael Frost who in the nineteen-sixties spent eight years of his spare time entirely rebuilding his *Boadicea*. Originally built at Maldon in 1808, and still showing the chubby shape of that time, she is now well capable of celebrating her two-hundredth birthday, though not in her original form, for her clinker planking was replaced by carvel in an earlier rebuild in 1887.

Most of the restored smacks were of the smaller class, up to ten tons (including two, *Gracie* and *Skylark*, which started life as half-decked pleasure boats off Clacton Pier, and the *Fanny*, an intruder from the Solent which celebrated her centenary in 1972). They range from the *Quiz*, launched at Paglesham in 1872 and re-launched in 1982 after being totally rebuilt at Woodbridge, to the *Peace*, built in 1909 and one of the last traditional oyster smacks to be launched in Essex. During the nineteen-seventies it seemed as if the Tollesbury stowboater *ADC* would remain the queen of the fleet, at least in size. In the early nineteen-eighties, however, another remarkable restoration was completed. The fifty-foot *Sunbeam* was in fact laid down not as a smack but as a yacht by Howard of Maldon in 1887, but before she was completed she caught the eye of William Cranfield of Rowhedge, skipper of the great racing yachts *Valkyrie II* and *III*, who had her completed to fish in winter and to compete with such legendary Colne racing smacks of another age as *Neva* and *Xanthe*. She survived unrigged into the nineteen-seventies and was acquired by David Gowing, one of the pioneers of the Colne Smack Preservation Society, who started her restoration, a task completed after his death by John Rigby at John Milgate's Peldon yard.

Thanks to the long extension of their life as motor fishing boats a number of Lynn smacks and shrimpers have recently been restored to sail as yachts including *Freda and Nora, Telegraph, Unity, Mermaid* (formerly *Charles and Josephine*), *Hattie May* and *Lily May*. The *Nellie and Leslie* has been re-rigged as far afield as Bremerhaven in Germany. Former sailing craft still in use (some, if present trends continue, perhaps destined also for restoration) include *Queen Alexandra, Rob-Pete, Victoria, Charlotte, Sea Fish* and *Marguerite*.

Two Colne Fishery police boats, the *Prince of Wales* and the *Victoria*, together with her dinghy *Albert*, are still sailing not far distant from the waters they once patrolled. The smaller beach boats have been, unlike the smacks, largely neglected. Only the fifteen-foot *Pet*, built like many of her class by Bugg in a shed behind a pub at Sudbourne, near Orford, in 1902, has been restored complete with a dipping lugsail and long mizzen outrigger. The Maritime Museum for East Anglia at Yarmouth hold a Yarmouth shrimper which it is hoped that one day they will restore. Until then these characterful craft are represented by the *Horace & Hannah*, built in 1907, and soon to sail again after an extensive reconstruction.

The Lowestoft smacks have been less favoured than their West Country counterparts at Brixham, but one example, *Gratitude*, owned in Sweden, won the Tall Ships race in 1976 and another, *Excelsior*, built in 1921 and thus one of the last of the line, is being restored by a trust based on Yarmouth and Lowestoft, where it is hoped she will lead an active life, more than replacing the former Yarmouth steam drifter *Lydia Eva* which, restored by the Maritime Trust, lay alongside the quay in her home port for some years. She was later removed to a museum site in London where she lay close to the coasting barge *Cambria*.

The conclusion of the classic Thames and Medway barge matches in 1953 also seemed like the end of a tradition. And so it was, but again it marked the beginning of another, for in 1962 barge-owners at Maldon, the chief home of the revival, restarted the Blackwater Barge Race which intermittently had been part of Maldon Regatta up to 1936. Not to be outdone, Pin Mill Sailing Club started a race the same year, thus giving Harwich its first sight of a barge match (with the exception of a couple of casual challenges) since 1857, though the whole tradition started there in 1844, nineteen years before Henry Dodd, "the golden dustman", founded the famous Thames race. The Maldon and Pin Mill races have continued annually, with the addition of events in the Medway and the Swale, and at Southend, and of passage races between the various fixtures.

The Colne Smack and Barge Race, started in 1971, is in many ways the most spectacular of all, providing as it does the sight of a mixed fleet of these traditional craft. This event is one of the achievements of the Colne Smack Preservation Society, which has its own little dock at Brightlingsea, where

The Whitstable "yawl" *Stormy Petrel*, originally a watch-boat, taking part in one of the annual Old Gaffers' races.   *Robert Malster*

members give each other moral and physical support in the restoration of smacks, and berth them when their restoration is complete.

Principally, however, the smack revival has been brought about by individual enthusiasts throughout Essex and Suffolk, many of them disenchanted by the characterless commercialisation of post-war yachts. I was considered mildy eccentric (at best) when in the mid-thirties I acquired the Mersea oyster smack *Charlotte*, for at that time and indeed throughout the nineteen-fifties it was generally considered that the only reason why anyone should wish to own any gaff-rigged boat was because he could not afford Bermuda rig, or was mad.

The bawley revival was later and more limited. The first example was the thirty-seven-foot *Bona*, Harwich-built in 1903 and re-rigged in the early nineteen-seventies when she was the only example to be seen. Others followed, and today the queen of this fleet is *Helen and Violet*, a Leigh bawley built by Cann at Harwich in 1906 and now owned at Brightlingsea. Her contemporary,

The *Marigold*, a perfect twentieth-century reproduction of a mid-nineteenth-century shrimper, almost ready for launching at Maldon.   *Barry Pearce*

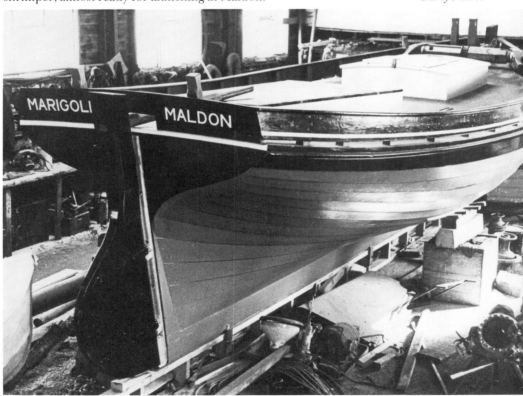

Auto-da-Fe, has been rebuilt but not yet re-rigged. Another once noted flyer, *Doris*, has also been rebuilt and re-rigged, as has the *Amelia Mary*, launched by Heywoods at Southend in 1914. As a cockleboat she was built with a centreplate, but this has not been replaced, yet she carries a generous sail-plan with confidence.

The renaissance has extended to the Rochester bawleys, worthily represented by *Thistle* and *Iverna*, and to the Gravesend version with the building in 1982 at Maldon by David Patient of the clinker-planked *Marigold*. She is a careful copy of the *Lillian*, built in 1862. The speed and sail-carrying ability of these beamy craft have opened the eyes of many smack owners brought up to believe there was no challenge to be feared from a bawley, with *Helen and Violet* leading the whole mixed fleet in the 1985 and 1986 Colne smack races. Perhaps the last word on this revival was spoken by an old Gravesend fisherman who attended the launching of the *Marigold:* "There's two things I never thought I'd live to see," he declared. "A dead donkey and a new bawley."

Smack racing is of much greater antiquity in Essex than yacht racing, dating back both in the Blackwater and the Colne to 1783. Mersea joined in the game in 1883 with its first recorded regatta, dominated by two smack races. None of these places can claim an unbroken annual tradition, but throughout the twentieth century West Mersea Town Regatta has opened with a smack race anually with only wartime interruptions. Such races have proliferated with the new interest in workboats, providing further opportunities for smacks and bawleys to race against each other, including Whitstable "yawls" such as the ex-watchboat *Stormy Petrel,* the *Rose and Ada, Gamecock*, two King's Lynn smacks, *Lily May* and *Mermaid*, and the Boston cutter *Telegraph.*

A great occasion for smacks and older yachts to compete with each other—also unknown in the early regattas—has developed in the Blackwater Old Gaffers' race started in 1963. The phenomenal success and growth of this annual event over the past twenty years has enabled it even to live down its lamentable name. No longer are the gaff-rigged boats the "tore-outs" or poor relations, for no event in the East Coast yachting calendar attracts a bigger entry or makes a braver show. And, though admittedly it is the grander and faster gaff-rigged yachts that have passed away, it is usually the smacks which are the first across the finishing line.

Even the little "winkle brigs", as the open clinker-built hack boats are known, have come into keen demand, chiefly from those who find a greater satisfaction in sailing them than more up-to-date boats which are smarter to windward and lighter in upkeep costs. Fifty years ago they were the mainstay of the Mersea Dabchicks Sailing Club, which has now for better or worse achieved the status of a yacht club. The "winkle brigs", however, continue the contest among themselves. The rules are few, for informality is the keynote, but any one which rigs a Bermuda sail is cast into outer darkness.

Meanwhile in Norfolk as early as 1949 enthusiasts acquired the hulk of one of the last of the sailing wherries, the fifty-year-old *Albion*, and re-rigged her to found the Norfolk Wherry Trust. After early success, attempts to keep her going in her traditional trade did not continue, and as in the case of the *Memory* she turned after a few years to the less problematical alternative of passenger chartering on the Broads. Soon she may have a sister, for in 1981 the restoration of the *Maud* (built at Reedham in 1899) was undertaken by Vincent Pargeter, Essex County Council's official millwright. The *Lord Roberts* has also been raised by the Norfolk Wherry Trust after concluding her career as a motor barge and then lying sunk for thirteen years. She has been presented to the Broads Authority for a proposed Broads Museum. Both these craft are clinker planked, and thus will be more representative survivals than *Albion* which uniquely was carvel built. The Wherry Trust example was followed in the nineteen-seventies by the Humber Keel and Sloop Preservation Society which restored to sail the

The wherry *Albion* negotiates a tight bridge hole on the Broads.
Roger Finch

steel keel *Comrade*, built in 1923, and the sloop *Amy Howson*, launched in 1914. The keel *Annie Maud* is preserved as a lively museum exhibit at York.

When current projects reach fruition, the renaissance of traditional craft will probably be at its peak. There are no more barges to be resurrected out of forgotten creeks, rescued from humble toil as unrigged motor barges, or saved from the humiliation of a static life as houseboats, while as age and misfortune take their toll the fleet is likely to decrease till probably not more than a score would survive into the twenty-first century. The smacks, being smaller and more economical to repair and rebuild, may in many cases extend their lives indefinitely with the example of the *Boadicea*, built in 1808 and still sailing, to follow.

Meanwhile, just as the furniture trade recognises its antiques and its reproductions, so imitations of traditional craft have begun to appear, some traditionally built (with a sensible application of modern glues and resins, synthetic canvas and cordage all of which the old-timers would have welcomed without reservation), and including Maldon smacks, a "Burnham bawley", a "Colne gaffer" and a Leigh cockler. Before many more years have passed devotees of traditional craft will not only be faced with trying to distinguish a smack built at Paglesham from a Brightlingsea boat, or deciding whether a bawley is of Leigh, Harwich, Rochester, or Gravesend origin; they will have to answer a question new to the waterside: "Is she a real one or a repro?"

The Sailing Craft   5

The Leigh cockler

THE PIONEER cocklers at Leigh a century ago found surplus naval galleys from Sheerness Dockyard a cheap and convenient form of craft, rigged with a boomless mainsail and foresail. These boats bequeathed their name to their purpose-built successors, which continued to be known as cockle galleys.

The work required a shallow craft, strong and flat enough in the bottom to be put ashore on the hard exposed Maplin Sands, but fast enough to reach the grounds before the ebb was too far spent. To meet these needs some new boats were built with centreboards—the only British workboats so equipped. Generally, however, the cockle galley developed into a smaller, shallower version of the carvel-built shrimping bawley, with the same topsail and bowsprit rig, but (like the cockling shrimpers of the Wash) with an open hold between the cuddy foward and the steering well aft. Most were about twenty-eight feet long, nine feet beam and two feet six inches draft, but by 1912 two were as long as thirty-four feet. The fleet, which in the 1890s numbered thirty-two, had by this time dwindled to about a dozen. Till 1911 they raced as a class at Leigh Regatta.

The cocklers' operations, on reaching the grounds, usually started with a good deal of prodding overboard with an oar to judge the nature of the sand—and as often as not an argument leading to a move elsewhere. The choice,

or chance, of place was all-important because, unlike other fishermen, the cockler could not shift if he did not like what he found. Once the galley grounded, there was time for a bite or a cup of tea before the crew tumbled overboard for six hours' hard raking till the tide returned. An iron-toothed implement, like a large garden rake but with a short handle, served to find the cockles just below the surface of the sand, and gathered them into piles. Then the "picker-up", a wooden bar with wire teeth, was used to scoop the heaps into a net bag in which they were washed in a convenient pool before being put into baskets. As three men could load two tons in a tide, it was no picnic, especially if they had to extend their raking more than, say, fifty yards from the bawley.

Back at the sheds, a dozen picturesque tarred wooden buildings beside the creek, the cockles were painstakingly steam-cooked, in a careful effort to avoid the ever-present risk of pollution, before going to market. Hundreds of tons were sent annually to London by rail. Huge deposits of shell on the foreshore are evidence of the scale of the industry, which was comparable both in technique and productivity with that in the Wash, but more consistent from year to year, because the Maplins, the Buxey and the Dengie Sands cover seventy square miles, of which twenty-seven square miles can be worked, against thirty-nine square miles in the Wash, with only nine square miles fishable, even though the Shoebury artillery range interfered with much of the best Maplins ground.

As increasingly powerful engines came to be used, it was found that the wash from the propellor could be used to churn up the sand and expose the cockles.

The peter-boat

THROUGHOUT most of the nineteenth century, London fishermen still made a living as far up the river as Greenwich and Woolwich, and even in the Pool. Their craft, which were to be seen everywhere down to Leigh, were peter-boats, little double-ended clinker-built open craft, sometimes fitted with fish wells. They had no cabins but rigged canvas tilts, known as "tilton-tails", through which the chimney of a tiny coal stove sometimes projected, gipsy-like.

They doubtless employed the simplest of fishing gear, a peter-net, a length of plain net, corked and leaded, along the edges of the tideway or across the mouth of creeks and outfalls, for such flounders or mullet as could survive the polluted water, and they also rigged these nets with pockets for taking eels. Another speciality was whitebait, a mixed fry of many species of fish, caught after half-flood in small stowboat nets fixed to the sides of peter-boats anchored in the tideway. The Whitebait Feast, which annually attracted leading politicians to Greenwich until 1894, recalls the tradition, as does the big Young Group of food companies, founded by William Young, the "whitebait king", who was at Greenwich till the end of the nineteenth century, when he moved down to Leigh. Flat fish were stored in shallow "pits" in the marshes at Leigh till there were enough for the peter-boat to make the voyage to Billingsgate.

The small upriver boats were content with oars, and those which were rigged chose a spritsail and foresail, as one would expect in the Thames Estuary.

These were close relatives of, and perhaps indistinguishable from, the pink-sterns, open double-enders eighteen to twenty-two feet long, which developed into half-decked or decked craft with gaff or sprit rig, topmasts and bowsprits. Such boats were built in the eighteen-thirties and lasted to the end of the century, but the first square-stern smacks, which developed into the bawley, began to appear at the same time and went on to replace them. Another variant in the gradual transition towards the bawley was the "pig-stern", which had a wide, deep counter as inelegant as the name given to it.

The peter-boat's counterpart in the Medway was the doble, a double-ender (probably the origin of the name) up to eighteen feet long with a miniature wet-well, rigged with a spritsail and foresail set flying. No thwarts were fitted; the rower would sit forward on a box. A few dobles preferred a lugsail and some of the last had a dagger board through the well. A remnant survived long enough to be fitted with motors; besides fishing they were used as watermen's boats.

The name peter-boat remains a puzzle; they may have been called after the patron saint of fishermen. On the Stour the name was applied to a type of small, double-ended unrigged fishing boat.

The bawley

IF THE name bawley is a corruption of boiler-boat, as seems likely, despite the rather unconvincing sound of the derivation, it cannot correctly be applied to smacks before the middle of the nineteenth century, when boiling aboard was introduced. But it has come to be used to describe all square-stern craft with boomless cutter rig, the type that became most commonly equipped with a coal-fired shrimp boiler in the hold.

The first of the type, at Leigh, were no bigger than the pink-sterns they were to replace. The *King William IV* has been acclaimed as the pioneer, a little four-tonner whose name conveniently dates her around 1830, the year of that monarch's accession. From that time both the fleet and the bawleys comprising it increased in size in response to the growing demand for shrimps by holidaymakers, and the availability of the London market by rail. Fish wells, not needed after the introduction of boilers, were soon abandoned, and as the shrimp fishery spread to Harwich, which became its centre in the twentieth century, bawleys thirty-five feet long, with a generous beam of over twelve feet, became the order of the day. As well as those built at Leigh and Southend, many were built by Cann of Harwich, and still more by Aldous of Brightlingsea, these two builders developing a deeper, finer hull with a beauty of its own. In 1890 there were eighty-six bawleys at Leigh, and seventy-two still under sail in 1913.

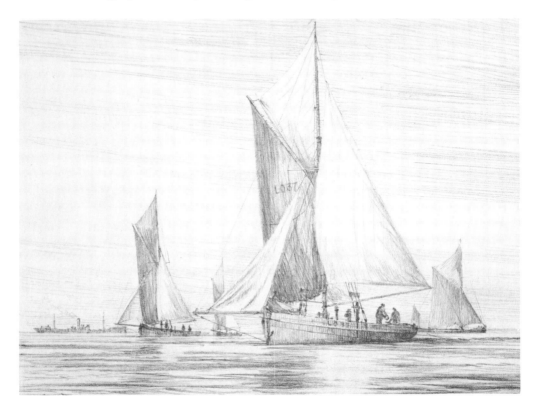

Southend had its own separate fleet of around twenty—always keen rivals of the Leigh men.

The Medway developed its own version, the chief differences being that the transom remained more vertical, the hold was divided to give a separate steering well aft and the mast set in a tabernacle for passing under Rochester Bridge for the smelt fishing in the upper reaches of the river.

The boomless rig was ideal for smacks which were miniature factory ships, processing their own catches. For such work there was much to be said for a wide deck which remained level in a breeze and was not swept by a low boom when tacking or gybing. Not all the other advantages often claimed for the rig can, however, be substantiated. A bawley could not be handled under topsail and brailed mainsail, as a sailing barge could, for the simple reason that a barge's sprit was controlled by vangs, while a bawley's long gaff could be trimmed on the wind only by the mainsheet exerting its tension through the leach of the mainsail. Nor was it often possible to reef the mainsail by luffing head to wind and shifting one block after the other to a higher cringle as the sail shook—particularly in weather which made reefing necessary! (The prudent method was to heave-to and hook in a handy billy tackle to control the leach as the blocks were transferred.)

More important, the long gaff and big topsail (hooped to the topmast and stowed aloft as in a barge) could never give the drive to windward provided by the extra couple of cloths on the leach of a sail setting to a counter-sterned cutter's taffrail. In an attempt to provide more canvas aft, some bawleys, including the *Auto-da-Fe*, started life with mizzens, which were evidently not found worthwhile, for the idea was short-lived.

The Essex oyster smack

THE SMALLER Essex smacks may be divided into two classes, those of twelve tons and over, which were used for stowboating and shrimping as well as for oyster dredging, and the little cutters of five to ten tons, which were employed on local oyster layings, some of them leading a long and busy life without ever sailing ten miles from their moorings. They were in the main small-scale replicas of the big rakish deep-sea cutters, even the five-tonners retaining channels for their shrouds, a feature dispensed with only in a few stowboaters which found them in the way when boarding the baulks alongside.

The style of their eighteenth century predecessors is shown by that remarkable survivor, *Boadicea*, clinker-built at Maldon in 1808 (though since rebuilt with carvel planking), a much chubbier form, which the nineteenth century builders refined into yacht-like counter-sterned cutters, though the locally built Maldon smacks were as a rule originally transom-sterned.

The great majority were built at Brightlingsea, by Root and Diaper, John James and most of all Aldous, who turned out a ten-tonner for £100, often trusting the buyer to pay him out of the first few years' work. Others came from Rowhedge, Wivenhoe, Tollesbury, Paglesham and West Mersea, and even one or two from Peldon, where there is no trace of an established yard.

Many of the later boats, at Mersea in particular, were of shoal draft, putting the ability to dredge in shallow water, or lie comfortably in the outfalls on "the Main" when winkling, above smart performance in sailing to windward. Indeed, when dredging under sail, making leeway was a positive advantage, for some of

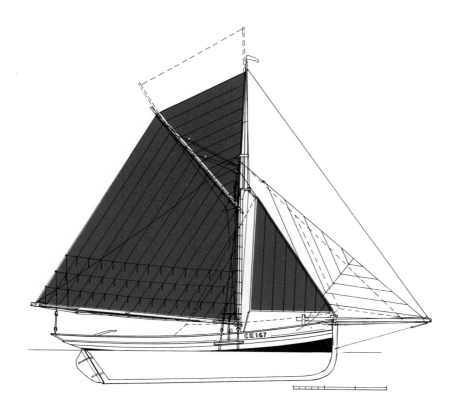

the deeper, smarter smacks lay hove-to like pilot cutters and covered less ground.

All were fitted with a wooden barrel windlass across the fore-deck, worked by hand-spikes. It was a surprisingly efficient piece of equipment and capable of breaking out an anchor under most conditions. Internal ballast consisted of iron scrap; iron fire bars were popular, although iron cannon shot, dredged up, was used and at least one smack carried a muzzle loading cannon, found in the trawl when dredging in the Wallet.

Trawl and halyard winches were seldom fitted in the smaller smacks, and most had forward cabins. The twelve-tonners rigged topsails, but few of the little oyster smacks found a need for them. Some were pole-masted; others had caps on the masthead in which a topmast might occasionally be rigged for such special conditions as a summer's dredging under the trees below Pin Mill on the Orwell.

Before the decline of the big oyster companies, a hundred smacks might be seen dredging in the Blackwater and nearly as many in the Colne. Dredging under sail continued until the Second World War, and thanks to the survival of so many smacks in this trade, their handy size and their fine sailing qualities, they have proved the most popular of all working craft for preservation as yachts.

The Essex deep-sea smack

THE VILLAGES of Rowhedge and Wivenhoe, tucked away up the tidal estuary of the Colne, developed a remarkable spirit of pioneering enterprise throughout the nineteenth century. The shipyards of Sainty, Harris and Harvey succeeded in producing some of the finest smacks and yachts in the country. The smacksmen ranged far afield, chiefly in search of oysters, and as their skill and daring gained recognition they were in demand as skippers and crews of some of the grandest craft in the age of the big yachts. This earned them money which in turn went into even finer and faster smacks. Brightlingsea, with the advantage of deep water at the mouth of the estuary, soon joined in, and throughout the latter half of the century Aldous's yard there was the biggest of all the Essex smack builders, turning out thirty-six big cutters of over twenty tons between 1857 and 1867.

Fifty-footers, with a beam of fifteen feet, were in demand as early as the beginning of the century, including *Adventure*, built at Rowhedge in 1814 (fifty-two feet by fifteen feet by eight feet), and *Indefatigable* (Wivenhoe, 1808, forty-one feet by fourteen feet by six feet). For registration, either the waterline length or the length "between perpendiculars" was measured; these smacks probably had counter sterns extending their overall length by some six feet.

The trend after the Napoleonic Wars was towards smaller craft, but some were an exception, the cutters reaching their zenith in *Aquiline*, built at Rowhedge in 1865. She was sixty-five feet long with a beam of fifteen feet, drawing eight feet six inches when loaded to her full capacity of twenty-one tons. Her main boom was forty-five feet long and the bowsprit twenty-five feet

outward. This was the limit for a cutter's gear, and some were converted to ketches, occasionally being lengthened at the same time. A few were also built with ketch rig, including *New Unity* and *New Blossom*, both bigger than *Aquiline*.

In addition to a hand-spike anchor windlass, they carried a hand winch forward of the mast with four barrels for working halyards and running out the bowsprit, and another winch or capstan amidships, also hand-operated, for the dredge or trawl warps.

As well as voyaging anywhere between Friesland and Scotland for oysters, these big smacks fitted out for sprat stowboating in winter, and also continued the tradition of mixing cargo and fishing voyages, using their speed for fish carrying, bringing spring potatoes from St Malo and the Channel Islands, or even a load of coal from the Tyne or Humber.

They were also salvagers, cruising among the Thames Estuary sandbanks to earn rich rewards from the many wrecks there. One of the most noted of the Rowhedge salvagers, John Glover, in 1857 built his *Increase* (sixty-nine feet by fourteen feet by six feet) with a transom stern, perhaps because the long counter was too vulnerable to damage in this rough work, or perhaps because he had moved to Harwich, where this style of stern was the fashion.

In the early years of the nineteenth century there were a number of these deep-sea smacks at Burnham and a few at West Mersea, but by 1874, when the fleet reached a total of 132, most belonged to Brightlingsea, with twenty-nine at Rowhedge, twelve at Wivenhoe and eight at Tollesbury. There was still a fleet of fifty-two at Brightlingsea in 1890, but soon after this the deep-sea oyster trade was killed by poisoning scares.

The Harwich cod smack

THE ORIGIN, development and decline of the Harwich cod smack are recorded with unusual precision.

The Dutch domination of the North Sea, and the wars which ended it in the seventeenth century, left Harwich impoverished, with only three forty-ton smacks. In one of these, Captain Richard Orlibar in 1712 fitted a well—not an original invention, for the Dutch had long kept fish alive in a section of the bilge with holes in the bottom between watertight bulkheads, and such craft are earlier mentioned both at Yarmouth and Brightlingsea. But Orlibar's venture revolutionised the cod fishery, especially after his son Joseph started working the well smacks in 1766 on the Dogger, at that time still largely a Dutch preserve. Instead of being an unpalatable item of dried, salted ship's stores, fresh-killed cod became a delicacy in demand for the tables of the gentry.

By 1730 the Harwich fleet had increased to twenty-four, six of them owned by Nathaniel Saunders, who made a contribution almost as important as that of the Orlibars by introducing a co-operative system of ownership known as "Bottomry". Sailmakers, ropemakers, boatbuilders and other marine tradesmen

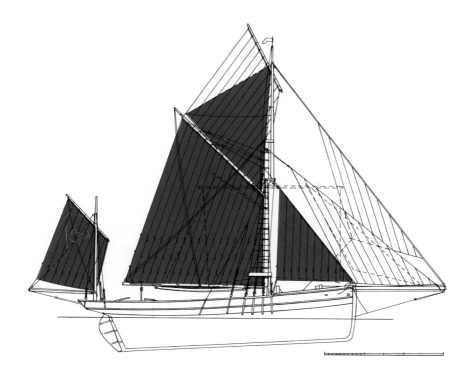

held Bottomry Bonds, which did not provide for a share in profits or losses but yielded a fixed rate of interest. Largely thanks to the capital produced by this mortgage system, the fleet reached seventy-eight in 1792—only to be almost totally destroyed by capture and enforced idleness during the Napoleonic Wars.

Efforts to rebuild it after 1815 failed. Saunders' grandson, in despair, left Harwich for Billingsgate and the trade passed first to Gravesend, Greenwich and Barking, and finally to Grimsby. A few traditionalists struggled on at Harwich, still voyaging to Iceland each summer into the early years of the twentieth century to fish with hand lines worked over crooks known as "tomboys", set in the weather rail of a smack lying "a-croke", or hove-to with headsails down and boom guyed out to leeward.

The early smacks were portly cutters, often built at Ipswich. They grew progressively longer and more shapely, adding a dandy's mizzen as the cutter's boom became too long for comfort, and the last were ketches. Some of the nineteenth century craft were built by Vaux of Harwich at the former Navy Yard, others at Aldeburgh, where, rather surprisingly, the fishery lasted as long as at Harwich, though the smacks worked with the Harwich fleet and returned home only for repairs or the Christmas lay-up. The other associated centre was Manningtree, where the Howard family owned fifteen smacks in the early nineteenth century. They were the first to see the possibilities of the new developments at Grimsby, to which their surviving fleet of eight smacks sailed in 1851, helping to found the fortunes of that port and of many of the men and boys on board.

The spritsail barge

A S THE lone survivor of all the commercial sailing craft on our coast, the spritsail barge earned its unique place by the combination of a simple hull, capable of adaptation, and a rig which could be handled by a crew of only two. She developed from the undistinguished flat-bottomed, shovel-ended, scantily-rigged Thames lighter to a thing of power and beauty. This was a change stimulated by the industrial growth on the shores of the Thames Estuary and the growing need to redistribute the bulk cargoes which poured into the Port of London.

The wealth of pictorial evidence available from illustrations of London's tideways and the East Coast harbours over the years enables us to trace with fair accuracy the changes that took place in the sprittie's hull and rig to its final perfection. In evaluating this evidence, however, it must be remembered that examples of the simplest type survived for a particular trade alongside those barges built, rigged and fitted out in the most advanced manner for their generation.

A simple sprit mainsail and foresail was adequate for the earliest barges, but by the opening decades of the nineteenth century topmasts were carried and bowsprits which topped up were fitted to enlarge the sail plan for estuary trading. It would seem that the shovel or swimmie bow and budget stern, despite

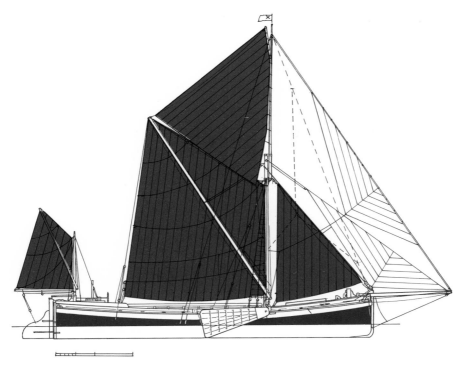

its economy of construction, was replaced in the eighteen-forties by a rather more conventional but still unusual "snib" bow, where the forward rake of the stem post was such that it indicated a compromise rather than a complete change from the traditional form. This lasted only a short time and the fully modelled round bow became standard, combined with a narrow transom stern, within a decade. An increase in length necessitated a mizzen mast and sail mounted on the rudder-head to assist the turn when going about.

From the earliest days the barge's sails were dressed with a preservative of cutch and grease, brushed on at yearly intervals to give the sails a characteristic russet-coloured sheen, shedding water and protecting the mainsail from the abrasion of the ropes as it was brailed up. The main brail was handled on a winch incorporated in the wooden mast case. With the tendency for ever larger barges to be launched, labour-saving devices were constantly adopted to handle the heavier gear. A separate winch was fitted to handle the main brail, iron mast cases became standard, and the primitive windlass at the bow, worked with a handspike, was replaced by one with heavy wooden bitts and geared so that it was possible for one man to heave up the cable. We can date the first introduction of wheel steering and the consequent repositioning and enlargement of the mizzen to 1873, when the *Anglo-Norman,* the barge which introduced it, was launched. By then leeboards were worked from iron crab winches on each quarter, replacing rope gun-tackles, while aloft hinged iron crosstrees replaced the older and more easily damaged wooden ones.

The spritsail stack barge

THE STACKIE was the barge of the rivers Blackwater, Colne and Stour.
While one may find abandoned quays on the Orwell, Deben and the Alde, it
was from the Essex rivers primarily that hay and straw were shipped up to
London and the London mixture (as the sweepings of the streets and the stable
clearings of the Metropolis were known) was returned to enrich the fields.
Although the characteristics of a spritsail barge expressly built for the trade were
not easily recognisable to the novice, a bargeman of the older school could always
identify them. They were flattish in profile, for their trading was within estuary
limits, and they were unlikely to encounter heavy seas. Their beam was generous
and their sides had little flare, to give them extra stability with a fourteen-foot
stack of straw or hay loaded aboard. Their decks were wide so that a full bale of
straw could be rested on the rails and provide an inward cant to the successive
tiers as they were loaded aboard from carts on the quay.

Aloft their rig had what the bargemen referred to as a "spinnakery look". It
was characterised by a long sprit and a tall topmast. When the last load of straw
was stacked aboard the mainsail had been so reduced in size by reef points
(another sign of a stackie) that it required a high peak to the sail for it to retain an
adequate driving force. The foresail was replaced for stack work by a much
smaller version, with a leach only half the length of a normal sail. A second set of
cleats, half way up the shrouds, to belay the running rigging was another sure
sign of a barge regularly in the stack work. The main brail was led forward to the
dolly winch on the windlass bits, while the sheet of the mainsail traversed a wire
substitute for the wooden horse submerged beneath the cargo.

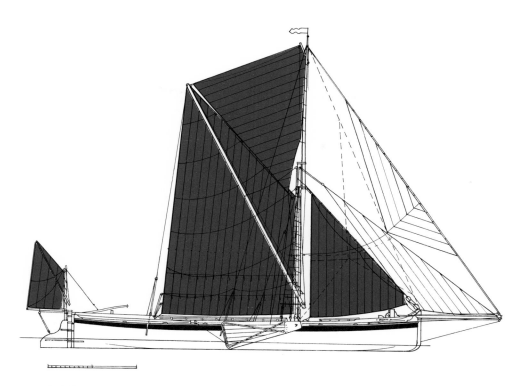

While stack barges remained faithful to the combination of a mizzen mounted on the rudder head and a twelve-foot oaken tiller long after the little Kent brick barges had changed to wheel steering, the Essex men invariably fitted a bowsprit and set a jib on it regularly. They needed all the sail they could carry on what was often a thrash to windward when they were London-bound. Having tied up at Essex tiers, as the mooring buoys at Woolwich were known, they could use the bowsprit topped up for setting the bridge sail when they worked their way up to Vauxhall, gear lowered down into a slot cut in the stack.

Stack work reached its height in the opening decade of the twentieth century. It continued until the last cargo of fodder for the railway dray horses was loaded at Erwarton on the Stour in the nineteen-thirties by the *Blubell*, a companion of the miniature stackie *Cygnet*. After a chequered career the *Cygnet* has survived as a barge yacht, and she is typical of a number of these little "farmyard barges" which scurried about the Essex and Suffolk rivers, only rarely venturing out into the estuary.

A brief revival of stack work occurred after the end of the Second World War, when baled straw was transported by barge across the estuary from the Colne to the Kentish paper mills. Although much of it was done by auxiliary barges, two purely sailing craft, the *Lady Maud* and the *Lady Mary*, gave the astonished crews of yachts and motor coasters the last chance to see a stack of straw working to windward under sail.

The mulie barge

THE BASIC spritsail rig is a primitive arrangement, and like most simple technology it works excellently within clearly defined limits. These became increasingly apparent once a spritsail barge was at sea and found itself facing severe conditions. The long sprit could produce a pendulum effect as a barge rolled in a seaway or lay at anchor in an open roadstead. Even when it was carefully stowed, the windage of the canvas aloft could cause problems when the barge lay wind-rode. The vangs, which controlled the extremity of the sprit, suffered cruelly as the barge lurched and pitched at her anchor, putting an almost intolerable strain on the falls and the iron straps which secured them to the hull. The failure of only one shackle could precipitate the sprit's breaking or worse. The development and adoption of the mulie rig was an attempt to minimise these disadvantages and yet retain the economic benefits of a spritsail rig for coasting work.

By stepping a ketch barge's big gaff-and-boom mizzen well forward of the wheel and cutting the sail plan to the same proportion of mizzen to mainsail as a ketch, it was found that a spritsail barge loaded with two hundred tons or more could trade coastwise throughout the year and show a profit. This change in the traditional sail plan of a spritsail barge would have been ineffective if it had not

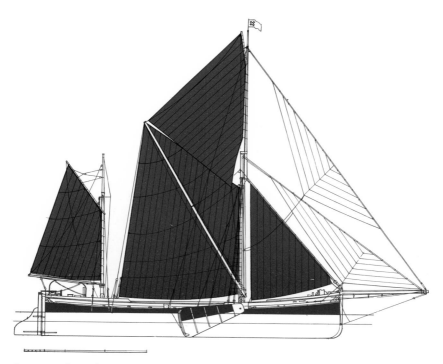

been for another innovation. The first mule-rigged barges appear in the eighties, and it is not a coincidence that this period also saw the general adoption by smaller sailing vessels of flexible steel-wire rigging. Prior to its introduction, the crews of sailing coasters were kept busy improvising cats'-cradles of preventer back stays, spanish windlasses and bowsings to compensate for the stretching and straining of the traditional hemp rigging during heavy weather. Keeping a sixty-foot sprit safely aloft before the days of wire rigging would have tested the skill of even the most experienced old-time skipper.

The first barges to be mule-rigged are difficult to trace, for the Custom House officials who kept the registers never found an official title for them. However we can say that an early example of this rig was the *Una*, built at Harwich in 1882. Most of the latter-day coasting barges were rigged as mulies. Notable among them were the four steel craft, capable of loading three hundred tons, the *Fred, Ethel, Alf* and *Will Everard*, launched by Fellows of Great Yarmouth in 1925 and 1926 for F. T. Everard. Two other steel mule-rigged barges, the *Aidie* and the *Barbara Jean*, had been built the year before at Brightlingsea for Ipswich owners.

The reduced size of the mulie's mainsail made it somewhat slower than a conventionally rigged spritsail barge of the same tonnage and less smart when working to windward in sheltered waters. But lying at anchor, sheltering from a gale in Yarmouth Roads or the Downs, with the gaff mizzen snugly stowed, with a shorter sprit and correspondingly smaller mainsail, the mulie certainly scored as the assembled fleet rooted and strained at their cables.

The boomsail barge

THE TRADITIONAL barges of the Thames Estuary built during the first half of the nineteenth century and intended for trading beyond sheltered waters were usually rigged with a gaff-and-boom mainsail. The earliest to be employed by East Coast owners, such as the *Industrious Ann*, working from the river Alde to London in the eighteen-hundreds, were cutter rigged. The addition of a small mizzen, set up on the rudder head, was encouraged as the barges began to be built longer, and it was found that unlike the shorter cutter-rigged craft they did not come about easily, particularly at sea when tacking. Indeed as the earlier examples, such as the *Industrious Ann*, were swim-headed, it must be wondered how they ever managed to work to windward at all. It required a mizzen sail to assist in bringing the barge's head into the wind and then to pay off again on the new tack with any certainty. The seventy-foot hull was tiller-steered, and the long boom, fully forty feet from jaws to the outer end, must have caused difficulties at sea as it swept low across the deck within striking distance of the helmsman.

Yet these barges, with only a few inches of freeboard and nothing more than a foot-high rail amidships, are authentically credited with regular voyages not only along the East Coast but far beyond. They carried Roman cement, packed in barrels in those days, from Sheerness and Harwich and loaded awkward logs above and below decks for the South Coast ports, returning with wheat or stone blocks. They did beach work, discharging bricks from Kent into carts as they lay

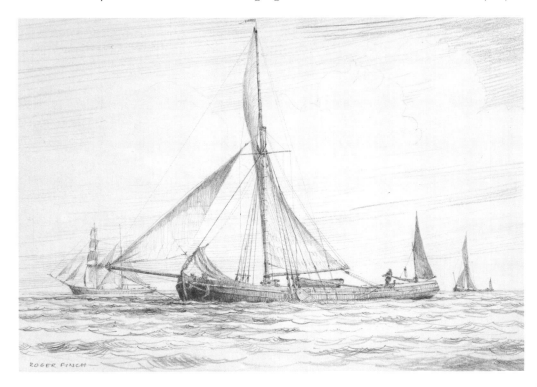

ROGER FINCH

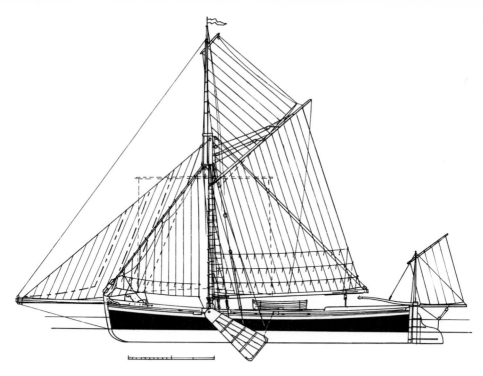

on the foreshore at Walton and Whitstable. Coal from the north-east ports was brought down to be discharged on the riverside hards of the East Coast rivers in the summer months, and it was not difficult to find a wheat cargo to make the voyage doubly profitable. Although boomsail barges could and did sail without ballast, it was unusual to undertake a long voyage without a cargo below hatches. This was of course at a time before the Board of Trade began to differentiate between those vessels deemed to be capable of trading beyond Estuary limits, i.e. the North Foreland and Orfordness, and those that were not.

The boomsail barges and their crew of three were typical of the small traders which belonged to an age before such well-meant regulations. Their leeboards were worked from tackles leading to each quarter and the primitive dolly winch at the foot of the mast served both to sweat up the halyards and to handle cargo. The mainmast rested in a heavy iron-bound wooden tabernacle, supported by heavy hemp rigging that sagged woefully after each blow, while their flax sails hung ill-fittingly. A bowsprit which steeved upwards, well out of the way when in a dock, was not yet universal, and a spar which ran inboard was equally common. While the foresail worked across a wooden or iron horse, the main boom was sheeted to a chock, bolted to a beam just abaft the main hatch coaming. The mizzen could be either a simple spritsail or a lug, sheeted to a heavy barn door of a rudder.

It is perhaps not surprising that the spritsail replaced the gaff-and-boom rig on barges that were launched after the mid-nineteenth century and that after a short period of experimentation with a yawl rig on larger hulls, the ketch rig, with its more equable distribution of sail area, was adopted for coastwise trade.

The ketch barge (square topsails)

WHEN the first ketch barges were built in the eighteen-fifties the ketch rig had only recently appeared. The traditional rig of the sailing coaster on the East Coast had been the brig and then the topsail schooner. The ketch was cheaper to rig and to maintain than the contemporary schooner, she could be managed with a smaller crew, and many seamen considered that a well-designed ketch was easier to work in almost any circumstances than a schooner of the same tonnage. The earlier ketch barges were rigged with a square topsail and occasionally topgallants, partly due to an innate conservatism but also to ease the work of the helmsman when the wind was aft of the quarter.

The first ketch barge launched at Harwich, and probably the first built on the East Coast, was the *Stour*. She was launched by Vaux of Harwich in 1857 and owned by him for many years, working in the coal trade, before passing to a Newcastle owner. She was originally fitted with a deep single topsail. The first builders of boomies complemented the square topsails aloft with a bowsprit and jibboom forward, while a topmast was carried on the mizzen. The crew required to manage the rig could number as many as five, but they were kept fully employed in port discharging the coal cargo, the usual trade for these big boomies. The ketch barge's main advantage over the older brigs and brigantines lay in the fact that, to sail effectively, they did not require ballast which had to be bought and then disposed of.

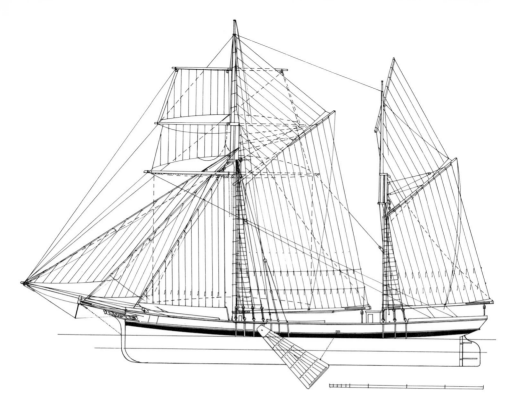

This bigger class of ketch barge, and the largest were capable of loading between two hundred and two hundred and fifty tons, was originally tiller steered. The first to be fitted with wheel steering was the *Alice Watts*, launched in 1875 at Ipswich. Although she and most of her contemporaries did not have a wheelhouse, a galley was usually carried on deck, strapped down in such a way that it could be unshipped when a deck cargo was loaded. A heavy windlass, worked by rocker arms, and known as Armstrong's patent, brought home the anchor.

A few big barges were built on the East Coast and were launched with even more elaborate rigs. The *Problem*, which did not have leeboards, the *Enterprise* which did, and the Harwich-built *Lymington* and *Parkend* were all schooners, although the latter ended her life as a ketch. Except for the *Problem*, which carried not only a topsail but a topgallant and set stunsails, all had double topsails and a few of the ketches adopted the same arrangement. A variety of schemes were employed to resolve the problem of combining a gaff topsail, set from hoops on the topmast, with square topsails. The upper yard of the lower topsail was either slung from a crane on the masthead cap or from a parrel which lowered down the length of the doubling. The upper topsail could be set from a wire jackstay set up on the fore side of the topmast. From the pictorial evidence which has survived, some ketches set a raffee upper topsail as an alternative, saving the problems and weight of a third yard aloft.

91

The ketch barge

THE ENTHUSIASM of builders and owners for jibbooms and square topsails on ketch barges faded in the face of experience. Although there were schooner-rigged barges built as late as 1890 and the *Goldfinch* was launched with square topsails in 1894, the vast majority of the boomies were rigged as straightforward ketches. By the eighties they were built on average of a somewhat smaller tonnage than the pioneers of twenty years before. They varied from big two hundred and fifty tonners, with counter sterns, drawing nine feet, down to craft which in every other way than their rig were identical to a modestly sized spritsail barge.

While it would be wrong to consider any one of them as typical, they could nevertheless be divided into two main groups, with the inevitable odd example which defies categorisation. The smaller ketch barges tended to be transom sterned; indeed some had been built as tiller-steered spritties, and while they had substantial rails, these were spiked on and were without stanchions, while the helmsman faced the elements without the benefits of a wheelhouse. Examples of these were the *Alpha, Byculla* and *Thalatta*. Most of them carried their boats on the hatches and had adopted roller-reefing on the mainsail by the time that they were either converted to spritsail barges, like the *Alice May, Mystery* and *Matilda Upton*, had met their end by stress of weather, like the *Mayland* and *Lily*, or were

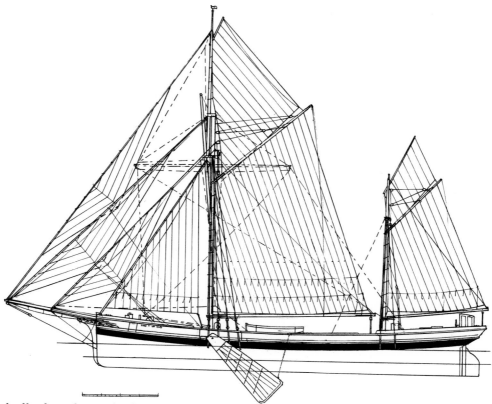

hulked at the end of a profitable life like the *Garson*. Some carried a running bowsprit or one that topped up, finding it more convenient than the fixed spar supported by a fiddlehead and setting the three headsails of their grander sisters.

These were built with counter sterns and usually loaded more than two hundred tons. They carried a yard aloft from which to set a square sail when running, and it was more usual for the bigger barges to set up their mainmasts with four shrouds rather than three, supplemented by a running backstay. Some steadied their mizzen mast with a temporary forestay from which they set a sail. Their bulwarks were built with stanchions, they carried a galley on deck and had a wheelhouse aft, like the *Genesta* and one of the last trading, the *Clymping*. Their size necessitated a heavy duty windlass operated by rocker arms so that if necessary the muscle power of four men could be brought to bear upon the anchor cable. The bigger ketch barges continued to work in the north-east coal trade until the very end. The *Sussex Belle* was lost in 1927 and the *Harold* in the following year, both coal-laden. Voyages to Saundersfoot on the Welsh shore of the Bristol Channel and to Dublin with malt were usual, and the continental Channel ports saw them frequently. Owners varied from a small syndicate of merchants, together with the skipper, to London proprietors, of whom Walker and Howard were the most prominent.

93

The Southwold beach boat

THE SOUTHWOLD longshoreman, like his brothers elsewhere along the coast, was in turn sailor, fisherman, shipwright and sailmaker, while his wife was net-braider and bait-gatherer and assisted her husband to cure and sell the fish that he caught in season. His workboat was of the simplest, for it had to be within the compass of his limited purchasing power, and to be light enough to be hauled manually through the surf and up the shelving beach when the catch was landed.

The longshoremen of Suffolk, where the beach boats for fishing were known as punts, and the southerly shore of Norfolk favoured a shallow transom-sterned clinker-built craft, between fifteen and twenty-one feet in length. Although a few were fitted with an iron centre plate, it was more usual to rely upon bags of shingle ballast stowed in the bilge under the second and third thwart. These were emptied upon landing, or alternatively they could be jettisoned at sea when the catch was a good one. The punts were lug-rigged with a long outrigger to starboard of the rudder head for the mizzen sheet. The big dipping lug mainsail was large enough to provide sufficient pull to the trawl when summer fishing for plaice and soles. The mainsail had five rows of reef points, and when reefed right down the iron traveller on the mast was hooked into a second grommet on the yard, aft of the one that was usually employed. The tack of the sail was then secured to a hook on the after side of the stem head;

ROGER FINCH

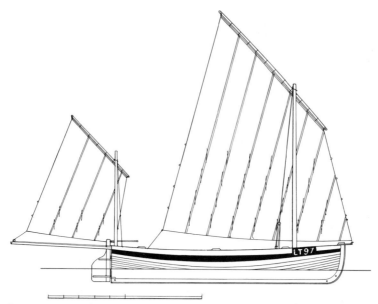

normally it was secured to a short iron bumkin which projected from the stem head. There were no shrouds to support the mast and the halyard, which was always set up to weather, and the sail down-haul, which was the only other rope, served this purpose. The mizzen was set off-centre to allow the tiller full play. This was often of iron and cranked to assist its movement.

The punts were rarely painted in the bright colours beloved by the Sheringham men but were white, tarred below the water-line, and only on the top-strake was a little touch of individuality indulged in with the use of blue, green and brown. They were built of oak and occasionally larch planks, on steamed oak frames, reinforcing fitted sawn frames, doubled at the floors on the larger boats, which carried the bottom boards. Pounds were fitted forward under the first thwart to take the catch. The bilge strakes were of extra thickness to sustain the heavy wear the punts were subjected to when launched and recovered. A crew of three was usual, and there were two pairs of thole pins each side for rowing when the winds failed. There was a subtle difference in build between the different groups along the shore, although this was blurred as boats passed between different owners. At Southwold, Critten's punts were rather straighter along the gunwales than those built by Reynolds of Lowestoft; he produced spratters with a subtle wave to their profiles. Double-ended craft of the smallest size, only a few in number, could be found alongside the conventional shaped punts, and these were rowed rather than sailed.

Colonies of beach boats fished from a dozen places along the shore north of the Deben. Besides Southwold, which had the advantage of a rail link to send away catches, there were similar groups of craft further south at Dunwich and Aldeburgh. Northwards, Kessingland beachmen were in the position of being able to sail a catch to Lowestoft, while those at Caister and at Hemsby could land a catch at Yarmouth fish quay.

The Norfolk and Suffolk beach yawl

THE BEACH YAWLS were the magnificent open workboats used by the Norfolk and Suffolk beach companies. The companies were independent associations of longshoremen, bound together by rule and tradition, based on the coast at a dozen places from Mundesley in the north down to Aldeburgh. The greatest concentration was to be found on the beaches adjacent to Yarmouth Roads, which lay between the shore and the Scroby Sands. In the days of sail, the Roads provided a limited but nevertheless very welcome shelter for the scores of vessels which sought refuge from gales and head winds, and the yawls serviced the accumulated fleets.

The yawls were of two types. A beamier version carried out stores and replacements for lost ground tackle; in summer they swept for anchors and didled for coal from submerged wrecks, victims of the winter's gales, while in autumn they were pressed into service to land the herring catch. The more majestic versions raced out with pilots and important supplies, put passengers aboard waiting vessels and were employed on salvage work on the offshore banks. Here weatherliness and speed were of prime importance. These thoroughbreds had been originally three-masted, but by the middle of the nineteenth century they had followed the trend set by the fishing craft of leaving their mainmast ashore. They compensated for the loss of canvas by setting a huge twenty-two-cloth lugsail on the foremast, dipped round the mast when going about, and a proportionally large mizzen.

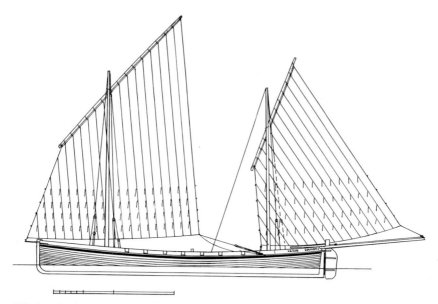

Clinker built and double ended, with an almost vertical stem and sternpost, the yawls were planked with some fifteen strakes of American oak on either side and averaged between forty-five and fifty feet in length. The beam-length proportion was about one to five. There were thwarts for eight oarsmen and also beams known as "dowsings", fixed at gunwale level, to which the iron mast-clasps were bolted and the mizzen "outligger" clasp was attached. All were strongly kneed-up with oak crooks. To sail effectively the yawls required a well-drilled crew of up to twenty, so that the big fore lug could be handed and quickly shifted round the mast, while the sacks of shingle ballast were pitched from one bilge to another as the yawl went about. In a light breeze, oars were shipped to assist in paying off on a new tack.

Two eyebolts were fitted amidships on either side of the gunwale and the foresail sheet-block hooked to the leeward one. The sheet was never made fast, but hand-held with two or three turns passed round a samson-post set up in the tabernacle which replaced the former mainmast. The mizzen sheet had to be slackened right off every time the yawl surfed on a big sea to prevent broaching-to. An eyewitness stated that "When off the wind, water was six inches above the lee gunwale and only trickling in, owing to the speed of the boat, although when going to windward, it would be necessary to have four men baling with buckets."

The yawls appeared regularly at regattas held at Yarmouth, Lowestoft, Pakefield and Kessingland, where companies competed from all the stations along the East Coast. The last race was held at Lowestoft in 1901. With the day of the sailing coaster over, particularly the sailing collier, the yawls were dispersed. Some of the smaller, full-bodied craft were sold to become pleasure boats, fore-and-aft rigged, working off the Essex beaches. Others became houseboats on the Broads.

The Yarmouth lugger

THE LUGSAIL rig was synonymous with the great herring fishery for most of its existence under sail, and traditionally Yarmouth was the home port of both. Luggers of a similar type were owned at Sheringham and sailed from Lowestoft and Southwold, and all had been originally rigged as three-masters. The mainmast was discarded before the middle of the nineteenth century, a change usually explained by the necessity of allowing more deck space for shooting nets and then clearing them of fish when they were hauled. Perhaps the change was related to the introduction of cheaper machine-made cotton nets introduced at that time, enabling smaller luggers to carry the same amount of fishing gear as the three-masters had done previously.

The great virtue of the lugsail is its simplicity. It requires little running rigging, and the old loosely woven hand-made canvas, unsuited to the finer skills of a sailmaker, could be used to produce a sail which served well enough. The lugsail is said to give a buoyant lift to the hull, and it can be stowed away easily when the decks are cleared for fishing. Its only disadvantage is that it is an awkward sail to deal with when tacking. The big crew on a fishing vessel, numbering at least eight and as many as twelve on a Yarmouth lugger, was able to handle this easily.

The usual drill when going about was to lower the yard, release the tack from the iron bumkin at the stemhead, pass the sail round the mast, and then secure the tack and change the sheet. These luggers carried foresheet tackles, secured outboard on both quarters, and the appropriate one was hooked to the sail before it was re-hoisted. The tail of the sheet could then be heaved in by hands working amidships.

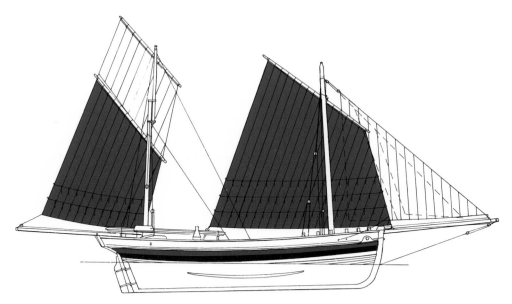

When fishing, the foresail was lowered and stowed to port, the foremast descended into a massive wooden support amidships, called the mitchboard, which was also used to secure the heel of the bowsprit, while atop the board a lantern glowed to give warning when the long wall of driftnets had been shot. The mizzen was replaced with a smaller "drift mizzen" of heavier canvas. A peculiarity of the herring drifter was that the mizzen mast was set well off-centre to port and required an iron bracket extended from the deck to provide sufficient tension for its rigging. The halyards and the burton which gave extra support to the masts were always set up to windward. A peculiarity of the East Coast luggers was that six robust timber heads protruded above the rail on either bow. These, with a cleat bolted on their face, provided belaying points for the rigging associated with the foresail and jib.

When the nets were hauled, a conical capstan, standing amidships in the centre of a walk marked by wooden treads, was used. While the hawseman stood near the bow casting off the buoys and seizings of the nets as they came aboard, the four capstan men trudged round, bent to their bars, hauling in the net warp. The rest of the crew did their best to clear the fish from the nets, one man stationed with a didle-net to catch any that fell into the sea as they came inboard. The catch was then sprinkled with salt—roused—as it was stowed below in the hold.

The hard nature of their calling soon wore the luggers out or sank them. Several were lost sailing salt herrings across the North Sea, and there were cases each season of drifters limping home after the sea had made a clean sweep of them. By the eighteen-eighties most of them had either been replaced by the superior carvel-built gaff-riggers, especially those from Lowestoft, or had adopted a loose-footed gaff mainsail and exchanged their wooden capstan for an iron patent one requiring less space and fewer hands.

The Lowestoft sailing drifter

WHILE many of the ports down the eastern coast of Britain in the days of sail had their fleets of herring drifters, none were built and rigged with as much distinction as those owned at Lowestoft during the last two decades of the nineteenth century. The introduction in 1884 of the steam capstan, invented by Elliott and Garrood of Beccles, to haul in the nets made it economic to build larger vessels than the old luggers, and an average length of about sixty feet became normal. The older luggers had been clinker built, with only their topsides doubled for greater strength and to lessen damage when off-loading a catch into beach boats. The new drifters were entirely carvel built, with handsome round counter sterns and a deeper heel. The main and mizzen were both gaff rigged, and although the basic sail plan was modest, for the mainmast had still to be lowered when riding to the nets, it could be augmented to ensure that the catch could reach market as quickly as possible.

The main, mizzen and foresail were all provided with bonnets which could be latched on, while two types of gaff topsails known respectively as the jacky and jigger could be set on both masts. The former type was extended along its head by a jacky yard and the latter along its foot as well by a long jigger boom. With their topsails set, a drifter fleet sailing hard for home carrying in addition mizzen staysails and huge jibs set from the masthead to the bowsprit end presented a picture unique in the annals of working craft.

More prosaically, the steam capstan on deck made them as potentially useful for trawling as for drift-net fishing. The drifters that undertook this conversion in the summer months were known as "convertor smacks".

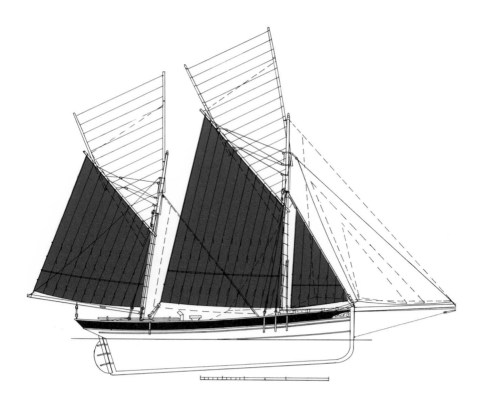

For the convertor smacks, trawling was not undertaken far from their home port, but the pattern of the herring fishery was dictated by the movement of shoals down the length of the North Sea and beyond. Some drifters went as far west as Penzance for the spring fishery, returning home in the early summer hoping for the appearance of the unpredictable mackerel shoals, caught with a broader-meshed net. Others coasted north to fish from Shields, then working their way south, landing catches at Whitby and Scarborough, finally sailed from their home ports for the three months of the main autumn herring season.

Lowestoft drifters were built by Capps and Crisp, and S. Richards, besides Fuller, who introduced the round stern. They could be distinguished by a taller mizzen which raked forward at an unusually pronounced angle. The mizzen masts of the Yarmouth boats built by Alfred Castle and T. Beeching were more upright and lacked the decorative gold finial of the Lowestoft drifters.

The end of the sailing drifter was sudden. In 1897 the first steam drifter built in East Anglia, the *Consolation*, was launched at Lowestoft, although she carried a full suit of sails. Her financial success proved beyond doubt the value of power and within six years one hundred steam drifters were working from Lowestoft. The last sailing drifters were built at Chambers' yard at Oulton Broad in 1900, the *Content* and the *Pretoria*. The *Strive* and the *Gwalia* were the last two sailing drifters to fish out of Lowestoft; the former became a yacht and the latter a pilot cutter.

The Lowestoft trawler

LOWESTOFT originated as an unimportant fishing station for beach boats. It was not until the end of a convoluted history of attempts to supersede Yarmouth as the entrepôt of the area by means of under-financed harbour-construction schemes that sailing trawlers began to work from the port, by then served by the railway; their number had reached 348 by 1876.

Two well-known builders were Richards and Chambers, who established yards on Lake Lothing. A trawler of forty-five to fifty tons was found to be appropriate to local requirements, somewhat smaller than the Humber smacks but more powerful than the "Brickies", as the Brixham craft were known. However, Suffolk fishermen were quite prepared to order new tonnage both from Devon and from Rye in Sussex. A Lowestoft smack usually had a fuller bow and a mainmast stepped further forward than the smacks built in Devon. Fullers, who had a yard on Lake Lothing, are credited with the introduction of the graceful elliptical stern which gradually replaced the square transom.

Lowestoft sailing trawlers were owned privately or by small syndicates. They worked independently, known as "single-boating", and were never dependent upon the steam-driven fish-carrier. An attempt to start a steam trawler fleet in 1890 failed disastrously.

A smaller class of sailing trawler, known as toshers, worked the fishing

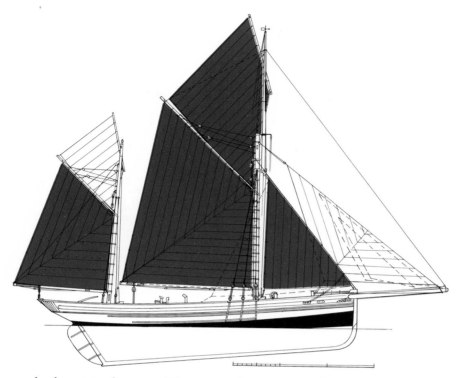

grounds closest to the port. They were about twenty-five tons and carried only three hands in summer and four in winter, when they shipped a cook; somewhat surprisingly this work was undertaken by the skipper in the calmer summer weather. They worked the area known as the Wold, inside the Haisborough Sand, off the Norfolk coast, and sometimes during the summer ventured as far as the Dutch banks. Some of the Wolders, as they were also known at Yarmouth, were convertor smacks which stuck to their trawling rig when steam had captured the herring drifting industry in the nineteen-hundreds.

So that the sailing trawlers could ensure a steady pull when fishing and then a fast passage home, an extensive wardrobe of sails was carried. Four jibs, of descending size, a big foresail of light, undressed canvas, a mizzen staysail and mizzen topsail could all be set in appropriate conditions. The mizzen mast of the Lowestoft trawler usually had a distinctive ornamental cap and a forward rake. The forward rake of the mizzen facilitated the heaving up of the cod-end of the trawl with a burton from the masthead. Another identifying feature was a gold stencilled decoration beneath the bowsprit hole.

A steam capstan with a vertical boiler was carried on all the larger Lowestoft sailing trawlers to assist in hauling the trawl, setting sails and anchor work. Though between the wars the port was increasingly used by power-driven fishing vessels a group of working sailing smacks survived longer at Lowestoft than anywhere else on the coast. As late as 1939, eight or nine were working regularly.

The Yarmouth trawler

BRIXHAM men and the fishermen of Thamesside Barking in Essex both lay claim to having invented the beam trawl for catching bottom-feeding fish. Paradoxically, the Brixham men had a fine harbour close to their fishing grounds but lacked an easily accessible market for their catch, while the Barking trawlers had the insatiable demands of the Metropolis at their back door but a long haul from the fishing grounds. New opportunities opened up with the discovery of the rich fishing to be had on the Dogger Bank. From the eighteen-thirties onward, the fishermen from both ports shifted their base. From Ramsgate, where a number of the Devon men had settled, there was a further migration to Hull, while Samuel Hewett of Barking moved his whole operation to Gorleston on the Yare in 1854.

Herring fishing was booming at Yarmouth, and with the establishment of a big fleet trawling was consolidated on the same scale. The arrival of the railway at the port in 1844 stimulated the whole fishing industry, but at first most of the catch from the four hundred sailing trawlers was dispatched by sea. Hewett pioneered the use of ice in the fishing industry. In the winter months it was collected from the frozen Broads and carried by sailing wherries to insulated ice-houses and then shipped aboard the smacks when they went "fleeting".

"Fleeting" implied that sailing trawlers remained on the fishing ground for at least six and sometimes as long as eight weeks, under the command of an "admiral", boxing their catch and transferring it in the smack's boat to the sailing

ROGER FINCH

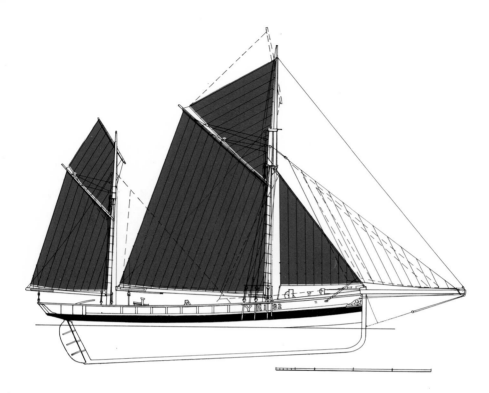

or steam carriers following the fleet. It was common for the smaller owners and the skipper-owners to attach themselves to larger fleets and to work with them. Unlike nearby Lowestoft, where there were usually trawlers that worked closer to their home port and returned every few days, Yarmouth smacks tended to be heavier both in rig and hull to survive weeks of winter weather on the North Sea. The eighty-two vessels of the Hewett fleet ranged between thirty-five and sixty-five tons net and were crewed by six men, working on shares. By the eighteen-seventies the ketch rig had been generally adopted, and they were fishing a trawl with a fifty-foot beam.

The replacement of sail by steam and the beam by the otter trawl began on the Humber at the beginning of the eighties. Within some fifteen years, sailing trawlers were a thing of the past at Hull and Grimsby. However, this revolution did not take place at Yarmouth and Lowestoft, with disastrous results for the industry.

Smacks built at Bideford, Rye, Wivenhoe and Ipswich sailed from Yarmouth. The dragging of a heavy trawl required a powerful sail plan and a deep, well-ballasted hull, most smacks carrying between twenty and twenty-five tons of ballast. The full rig of a trawler included a mizzen staysail and jackyard topsails on both masts, and in summer many shipped a mizzen topmast. The Yarmouth smacks were distinguished from their West Country counterparts by a fuller head, enabling them to carry their mainmast somewhat further forward, while they never attained the size of the Grimsby craft.

The Yarmouth shrimper

THE SAILING shrimpers of Great Yarmouth provide a striking contrast to the big "factory ship" bawleys of Leigh and Harwich. They were little clinker-built sloops, from nineteen to twenty-two feet long, with a beam of about eight feet five inches, though one, the *Mazeppa*, was twenty-six feet. They were decked only from the stem to a bulkhead to which was fixed a three-sided wooden mast tabernacle. This foredeck provided a tiny cuddy, with two lockers and a stove.

Only a single headsail was set on a bowsprit, there being no forestay to the stem head. The bowsprit forestay and a single shroud each side comprised the standing rigging. The setting of the loose-footed gaff mainsail was unusual, for the boom had no jaws, but extended forward of the mast, usually to starboard. A rope snotter spliced round the mast passed through a score in the end of the boom, and was made fast to a cleat on its top. This dispensed with the need for a clew outhaul, for the clew could simply be hooked to the after end of the boom, and the foot of the sail set smart by heaving the spar aft. It also allowed the boom to be unshipped and the mast lowered with the maximum ease. Possibly the boats had once been lug rigged, and a way was found to retain this advantage with the change to boom and gaff.

Throughout the last quarter of the nineteenth century there were some

ROGER FINCH.

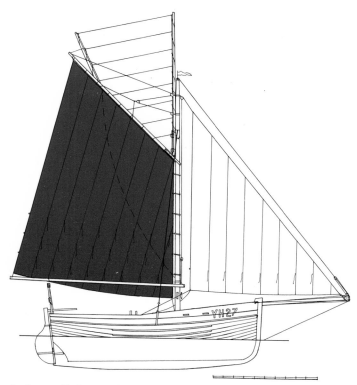

sixty-five of these little craft in various places beside the long Yarmouth quaysides, divided into South Enders, which lay along the quay above Gorleston, and North Enders, which moored above the Haven Bridge and in the North River and so had to face a long row up and down the harbour, including lowering the mast for the bridge.

As their boats were too small to accommodate a boiler, the Yarmouth shrimpers had to bring their catch ashore to be cooked in their own homes, in coppers already on the boil when they came in. Many of these houses sported brightly painted signs, with shrimp boards in the front room on which the shrimps were sold to the visitors. For this reason they preferred to work early morning tides, fishing in deep water some two miles offshore, often round the Cockle lightvessel. A century ago brown shrimps (which kept fresh longer) were favoured up to June, but later pink shrimps ("red 'uns") were fished all through the summer.

A similar but smaller shrimping fleet worked out of Lowestoft, but these craft seemed to have retained lug and mizzen rig, and not to have become such a specialist departure from the boats on the nearby beaches.

The Norfolk keel

ALTHOUGH they disappeared from the Broadland scene just before the advent of photography and it required an early example of marine archaeology to discover a reasonably accurate impression of their appearance, the Norfolk keels are worthy of inclusion in our list. They were the predecessors of the graceful wherry and closely resembled the medieval traders upon which the early outstanding prosperity of the region depended. The keels were indeed the last survivors from a very distant past.

An abandoned keel was dug out of the mud in 1912 at Whitlingham on the Yare, where it was supporting the river bank. She was found to have a length of fifty-five feet. and a beam amidships of thirteen feet eight inches, and drew about four feet. Old records indicate that the keels varied in size between twenty and ninety tons burthen, so the specimen excavated lay somewhere between these two extremes. This same keel was salvaged by a team of underwater archaeologists in 1986 and the remains were taken away for preservation.

Further evidence of their appearance can be gained from a study of the paintings of the Norwich School, topographical artists who sought inspiration from the Broads and the waterways on their doorstep in the first decades of the nineteenth century. Their paintings show that the keels were of a massive clinker construction, were built with a narrow transom stern and carried a single rather

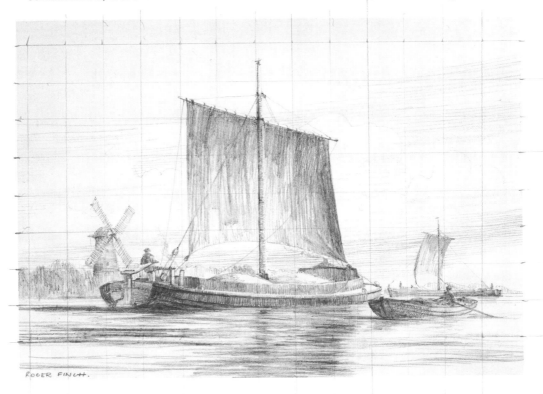

ROGER FINCH.

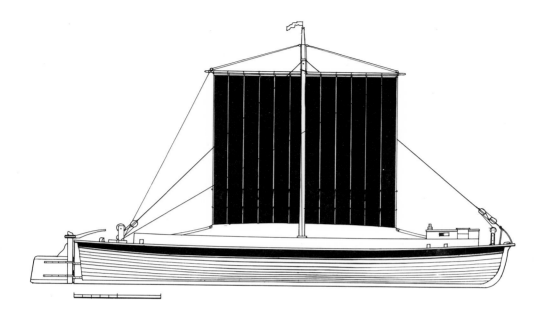

short mast, setting a squaresail. The mast was lodged between uprights amidships and arranged for easy lowering by a winch at the extremity of the bow. To accommodate the man at the winch handle, the covering board projected well beyond the stem to provide a short platform. Aft, a second windlass was fitted to raise the sail, and the lower of the two enormous halyard blocks was secured to a ringbolt a little forward of the windlass bitts.

Living accommodation for the keelman was situated in the bows, built up to give sufficient headroom. Its occupants shared its limited space with tar buckets, shovels and warps. However, they seldom lacked fuel for its iron stove. Coal was a basic cargo for the keels, loaded from the brigs lying at Yarmouth or out in the open roadstead, and then carried up the Yare to Norwich.

The sailing colliers demanded to be ballasted for a safe return voyage to the North. Ballast was lightered into the harbour by the keels from a shoal off the mouth of the Yare, and as many as six keels would load at each tide.

The black tar on the keel's hull below the waterline needed frequent renewal, and the accumulation of weed was burnt off, together with the old tar, by reed torches before a fresh coat was applied. The hatches were dressed with red oxide, and white lead paint for the bitt-heads completed the colour scheme.

Perhaps the most enduring work that we may attribute to the keel was the transportation of turf and peat, cut for use as an economical domestic fuel. It was the continuous cutting of peat over the centuries from the low-lying areas adjoining the rivers that created much of the Broadland we know today.

The Norfolk wherry

THE WATERWAYS of Broadland were the home of the sombre-sailed Norfolk wherry. Today the Broads are a popular holiday area, and it is difficult to believe that this intricate system of shallow waterways used to deliver cargoes of barley and bricks, malt from the riverside kilns, and coal for the village fires. The wherries loaded stacks of reed for thatching and fodder for the dray horses at Norwich; timber cargoes were piled on the hatches when the hold was filled and then cantilevered out beyond the width of the deck.

Their origin lay in the eighteenth century, when they carried passengers and delivered groceries, cargoes which were too valuable to be entrusted to the lumbering keels. It is probable that it was only with the introduction of machine-woven sailcloth at the end of the eighteenth century that a large and effective gaff sail of any size could be produced. The appearance of the wherry as a maid-of-all-work, as a direct competitor to the square-sailed keel rather than a craft specialising in passenger work, probably dates from this time. As the old wherrymen said, a good sail was more important than a good wherry.

The wherries varied considerably in size. Some, serving the upriver mills and maltings, were only thirty-five feet overall, loading some fifteen tons, and sailed by a single lad. The largest ever launched was the *Wonder*, which carried no less than eighty-four tons of coal. More typical would be a wherry of about fifty-eight feet, having a beam of fifteen feet, and drawing about five feet fully loaded. The traditional construction was clinker, which helped to produce a

ROGER FINCH

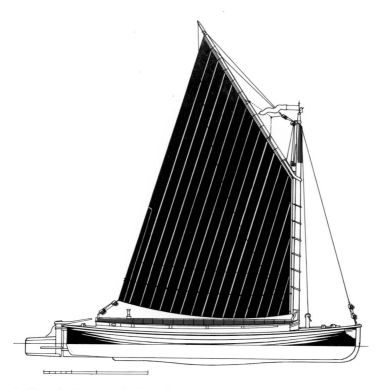

graceful, shallow hull and a hollow bow. The shell, usually of fourteen two-inch thick oak planks each side, was formed around two or three moulds, before the frames were built in and the deck beams fitted. A single hatch ran almost the length of the hull, terminating at the stern with a small cabin for the wherry's two-man crew. A narrow transom stern was common on the smaller wherries, known as the North River type, and helped to provide space for an adequate cabin.

The mast pivoted between massive oaken partners and was counterbalanced with a lead weight. This enabled it to be lowered easily and then raised again when negotiating bridges. The mast was unsupported by shrouds, and the gaff was hoisted by means of an ingenious combination of peak and throat halyards, which led to a winch at the foot of the mast. Another singular adaptation to river work adopted by the smaller wherries was a removable keel, which could be unbolted, and then moored to the river bank while the wherry negotiated the last few miles to her destination.

Wherry sails were always black, painted with a mixture of coal tar, herring oil and lamp black; alternate sides of the sail were dressed at yearly intervals. The masthead vane was individual to each wherry, and the frame, supporting a fathom of red bunting, was embellished by a painted metal silhouette of delightful invention. Dancing girls, Lord Nelson, suns and stars, mermaids and wheatsheafs all appeared. A fine collection of them is held by Norwich Museums.

111

The Norfolk fishing punt

BEFORE the First World War all the coastal villages along the Norfolk coast between Yarmouth and Sheringham had at least a few open boats for fishing and some as many as a score. All were launched from the beach and usually retrieved with the aid of a wooden capstan or an iron cargo winch salvaged from a wreck and anchored down well beyond the reach of the highest tide.

Northward from Yarmouth as far as Happisburgh (pronounced Haisbro') the beach boats were distinguished from their Suffolk equivalent by being double ended and known, possibly because of their exceptionally flat floors, as punts. They were not, however, like the crabbers of Sheringham, designed to be carried bodily across the wide beach at low water, but were conventional in build and shallower. Nevertheless, in common with the crabbers their sailing performance was improved by carrying shingle in small sacks to serve as ballast.

The punts were to be seen lined up between the yellow dunes and the sea, set up with a wooden "stool" under each bilge, ready to launch over greased wooden skids. Their neighbours were the last of the big beach yawls to which they were directly if humbly related, for a double-ended clinker-built hull is an ancient tradition on this coast.

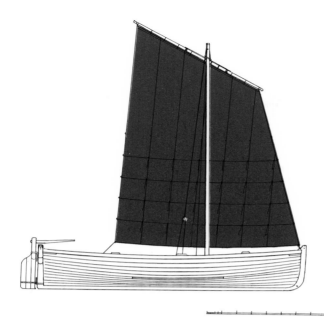

They varied between eighteen and twenty feet in length, with a six- to seven-foot beam. The upper limit of their size was imposed by the necessity of manhandling them down to the surf and launching.

The Norfolk punts were owned by families who regularly provided crews for the "big boats", the trawlers and drifters working out of Lowestoft and Yarmouth, and until the last decades of the nineteenth century crewing the beach yawls. A share of the earnings from a successful salvage operation or a fishing trip to the Dogger Bank or to Smith's Knoll provided the necessary capital to pay for a new punt or to replace worn out gear. Punts and smaller beach skiffs, pulling boats twelve to fourteen feet long, were frequently worked by old men and boys, with the stalwarts only participating between times spent at sea, away from their home village. It was seasonal work, with a variety of fish caught with differing nets and lines. The weeks between June and September saw long lines shot, buoyed and then hauled at break of day, while crab and lobster pots were set and collected after baiting with unsaleable fish. The advantage of a double-ended boat is apparent when working under oars, for it could be easily rowed astern. Autumn brought the sprats and required the smallest meshed nets. Those used to trap the autumn inshore herring shoal were larger and had a mesh of a fraction over one inch square. The "October herring", which swam close inshore within the limited range of the punts, although small, was full of fat and ideal for smoking.

Fishing was carried out under both sail and oar. The tack of the tall, rather narrow lugsail of the punt with its four or five rows of reef points was secured to an iron hook in the bow. When going about the sail was partly lowered and the yard passed round the mast, then the sail was reset. The lugsail is not best suited for trawling, but with the introduction of motors this became easier.

The Norfolk crab boat

THE HARBOURLESS shores of the North Norfolk coast were the home of small crab boats which up to the outbreak of the First World War had to be manhandled up and down the beaches. For this reason they were only about twelve feet on the keel and sixteen feet overall, and instead of rowlocks or tholes they shipped their oars through ports cut in the top strake, known as "orrucks"; when beaching the oars were used to control the boat's approach and secure in the "orrucks" they could not be washed out. The oars would be passed from side to side through the "orrucks" to serve as handles for lifting the boat.

They were symmetrical double enders, with bow and stern identical, and the wide strakes of their clinker planking were brightly painted in combinations of red, white and blue, with tar below the water line. The rudder projected below the keel and helped to give some lateral grip on the water. The rig was a single dipping lug, nearly black in colour, with the tack on the stem, but taken to a hook on the weather bow when running. Bags of shingle served for ballast, shifted to windward when sailing, and emptied out on beaching. With their simple construction, they were built all along the Norfolk coast, but those by Emery of Sheringham were specially highly regarded.

Similar boats a few feet longer, with a small cuddy forward, ventured as far as Southwold herring drifting, whelk potting and lining for cod. They were known as hovellers or "hubblers", and their crews as "hovelleers". The name suggests that they might once have been employed for tending on wrecks and retrieving ships' anchors, like the bigger beach yawls, but since there were no sandbanks off the North Norfolk beaches most craft were wrecked on the shore,

to the benefit of the longshore men and the Lords of the Manor. Another variation, which seems to have vanished in the mid-nineteenth century, was the pinker, said to have been used specially for cod lining, and to have had a more permanent cabin than the hubbler. The name presumably derives from some form of narrow "pink" stern.

In 1875 there were 150 beach boats at Sheringham and fifty-five at Cromer, reducing to seventy and twenty-five in 1914 as the developing holiday trade provided alternative longshore employment, and some Norfolk men moved away with their crabbers not only to Grimsby, which attracted so many fishermen from all around the coast, but to many smaller places such as Felixstowe and Whitstable. Sheringham and Cromer were always the chief centres, but there were also boats at Happisburgh, Bacton, Mundesley, Trimingham, Overstrand and Weybourne, working from the beach.

Since the First World War, motor crabbers, hauled up by tractors or winches, have adopted a deeper hull form, with less symmetrical ends, but the traditional double-ended shape and even the "orrucks" in the top strake have been maintained, perpetuating a type of craft that might well date back to the Middle Ages. The latest crab boats have been built at yards at King's Lynn and on the Norfolk Broads; a fibreglass version is also produced at Blakeney.

115

The billyboy cutter

THE TITLE billyboy was a collective designation given to the traditionally built seagoing trading craft of the Humber. Most were built and sailed from its southern shore. They regularly traded as far as the Thames and along the East Coast, and the smallest of the class were cutter rigged. These little craft perpetuated a style typical of the small traders of the first half of the nineteenth century.

They were always well known at the Wash ports, and several were built at Walsoken on the River Nene. They traded to Beccles and Norwich and were owned in Ipswich and Harwich before the spritsail barge, with its lower operating costs, replaced them. Traditionally the skippers made a home aboard their craft and lived with their families in the tiny cabin aft, a custom all too tragically confirmed by the contemporary accounts of their loss. To get the gaff aloft and the topsail set, a crew of three was needed, to be paid from the profit on a cargo of only a few score tons. No wonder the skipper-owners sailed with their families, who acted as unpaid hands.

They landed their modest cargoes of coal, bricks and, in later days, cattle food and artificial fertilisers at all the picturesque East Anglian harbours. In the

contemporary paintings of these scenes, they are easily recognisable, with their rounded ends, slab sides, clinker planking and generously cut sails.

The cutters' size belied the voyages they could make. Smaller versions were some forty-five feet overall, drew seven feet and loaded only forty tons, but regularly made profitable voyages to London. Inland coal from Goole on the Humber to the Thames and then a return freight of cement was a standby upon which most of the skippers, who were often part-owners, could rely. They were the last sailing traders, indeed the last commercial craft, to frequent the quays at Cley, Blakeney, Brancaster and the old beach jetty which once existed at Hunstanton.

The cutter-rigged billyboys scarcely survived long enough to adopt modern steel-wire rigging and the galvanised metal blocks of the spritsail barges. Their heavy hemp shrouds, varnished wooden blocks, loose-footed mainsails and topsails which were hooped to the topmast harmonised with the scraped and varnished main wale, which set off the brightly painted bulwarks and the cheerfully decorated cheeks for the anchor cable. A carved tiller and brass-bound cabin chimney, removable for canal work when the mast, set in a massive wooden tabernacle, was lowered, were matched with a primitive handspike windlass forward.

Although they were built with a conventional keel, their rotund lines and flat floors required the assistance of leeboards to make working to windward effective. Their shape was imposed by the demands of the locks on the Yorkshire waterways, and the almost vertical sides and semi-circular bows ensured that they could stow the maximum amount of cargo.

117

The billyboy (ketch and schooner rig)

WHERE the rivers broaden out and join the sea, the river trading craft tend to develop into a separate type, one which could make the best of both worlds. The billyboy ketches and schooners of the Humber estuary, which traded along the East Coast, exemplified this well. They were the seagoing development of the Humber sloop and its larger version, the billyboy cutter.

The older port registers, dating from the eighteen-fifties, referred to the ketches as "dandy-rigged", for the former term was not yet generally accepted. A few, such as the *Minerva* of Goole, were schooner rigged, with square topsails, while others like the *Blue Jacket* and the *Lively* had the foremast rig of a topsail schooner and the shorter mizzen of a ketch. This latter arrangement enabled them to be built with a long hatch amidships to assist in cargo work.

The square topsails of the ketches were generally arranged so that the topsail yard was raised and lowered on a parrel, sliding on an abnormally long doubling. A modestly sized topgallant yard was carried on a wire extending from the hounds to the topmast head, and the clews of the sail were permanently shackled to the topsail yardarms. The topgallantsail was furled by a seaman using the footropes of the topsail yard. The schooner-rigged billyboys did not always stow their foresail in the normal way, but kept the gaff aloft and brailed the sail up to the mast. A jibboom, which was shipped inboard when in dock, was usual in the older craft, while a bowsprit which steeved up was more common in the ketches.

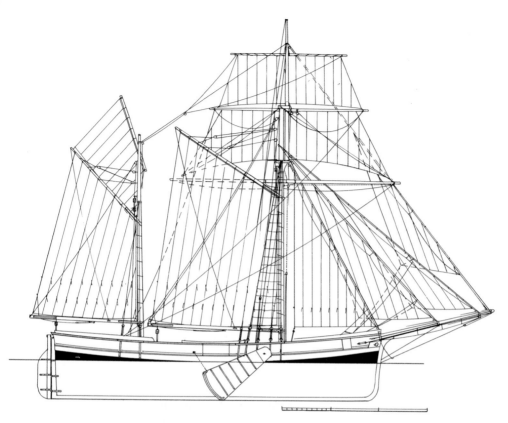

Like the little trading sloops of Suffolk and Essex, some had started life as sloops and had then been lengthened and re-rigged as either ketches or schooners. The *Only Son*, which was built at Leeds in 1861, underwent this transformation, and was later owned at Wisbech. One of the last clinker-built billyboys to trade along the East Coast was the *Evening Star*, built at Mexborough, far inland on the river Don, in 1873. She was run down by a steamer in the Wash in 1905, shortly after the *Eva*, owned at Southwold, had been lost in Robin Hood's Bay in 1903. The *Eva* was built in 1872 at Allerton on the Humber, not far from Knottingley, where there were four shipyards.

The hulls of the larger billyboys perpetuated the shape of their cutter-rigged predecessors, wall-sided and flat-bottomed, which made them well adapted for taking the ground. They were used for beach work on the Norfolk coast; one of the last in this employment was the *Ellis* of Lowestoft, built in 1858 and lost in 1920, still in the coal trade.

Like the spritsail barges they all had a long main hatch, and the masts of the ketches were set in substantial wooden tabernacles, carried down to the keelson. A heavy cargo winch abaft the mainmast was also used for setting sail. All except the largest billyboys had a simple barrel windlass in the bows, worked by handspikes. The boat was carried on the main hatch.

The Lynn yoll

THE LYNN yoll was one of several locally developed inshore fishing craft which were replaced by the end of the nineteenth century by the fashionable "cutter" hull, profoundly influenced by the Victorian yacht. Its name would imply a connection with the beachmen's salvaging boats, but the similarity was limited to a sharp stern. The yoll was similar in build to the Norfolk punt, sharp sterned, flat-floored and clinker planked, but built on a larger scale and usually thirty feet in length and decked. Like most of the East Anglian clinker-built craft, the individual planks were considerably wider than those used on the South Coast. Splines were fixed along the lands (the point at which the planks of the hull overlap) to provide smoother topsides over which to work the fishing gear, particularly trawls. It also minimised the damage craft might sustain when moored alongside.

Internally the hull of the yoll was strengthened with substantial bilge stringers and externally with bilge pieces to take the hard wear to which they were subjected when grounding on the mussel and cockle grounds. Their decks had a wide hatch amidships stretching from mast to stern similar to that of the shrimpers that replaced them. The yolls were shallow drafted, which enabled

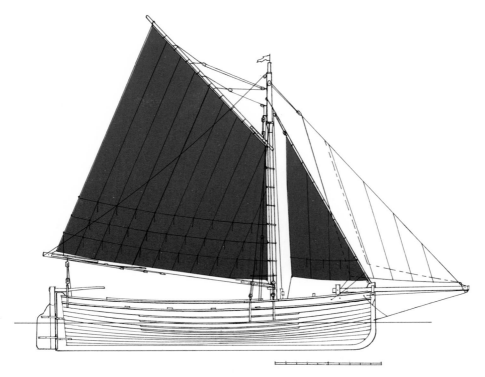

them to get on to the banks and dry out quickly, while their full bilge helped to keep them upright for loading.

They were used for shrimping, the shrimps being cooked aboard, but more importantly for working the mussel grounds to collect the "poor man's oyster". They grounded at low water and then as the tide flowed they would wallow back to Lynn or one of the smaller ports loaded with mussels or cockles raked up from the banks. Turning up the channels sailing to or from the grounds required the adaptation of an easily handled cutter rig with a long reeving bowsprit, set to starboard of the stemhead. With a prevailing south-westerly wind this allowed the jib to be dropped clear of the stemhead at the end of the day's work. A square-headed topsail was set on the pole mast in light weather and there were always enough hands to make easy work of sailing, for cockling required at least three hands.

A pair of sweeps was carried, "the wooden engine", to assist the yoll home in a calm and to ensure it went about in light airs. The sweeps were worked by men standing on the bottom boards. A single sweep was often used to ensure the craft went about, for no-one could claim that the performance of the yoll was equal to that of the neat cutters that succeeded them. It is interesting to note that the first of the locally built counter sterned shrimpers were clinker built, like the yolls. The change to carvel built, deep-heeled craft was not completed until after the turn of the century, for the yoll *Baden Powell* still survives, the very first craft built by the Worfolks of Lynn, before the brothers turned to the newer modelled shrimpers and smacks which made their name.

121

The Wash smack

THE OFFSHORE smacks of Boston and King's Lynn were big carvel-built cutters up to sixty feet long, distinguished by their round counter sterns. They carried topmasts but did not set their shrouds in the channels obligatory for most Essex cutters. Instead, their flush-fitting shroudplates were protected by external wooden chafing pieces. The anchor chain sheave was housed in a big wooden davit, perhaps because smacks working in such narrow and violently tidal channels needed a reliable anchor and a fitting which would not allow the chain to jump out in a heavy sea and shallow water, or perhaps reflecting their use as stowboaters.

The chief builders at Boston were Charles Thompson and his son Walter, Alexander Gostelow, much favoured for smack yachts in the nineteen-twenties, and Reg Keighley, with his sons, Rob, Ray and Dennis, who alone among the Wash builders carry on wooden yacht design and construction to this day. At Lynn, the Worfolk brothers came in 1901 from Knottingley, where their father was a schooner builder, to revive a trade which had largely died out locally, for of the thirty-five smacks of over fifteen tons at Lynn in 1900 only three were built there, and one each at Boston and Wisbech, the remainder coming from all parts of the country, including ten from Colneside yards. Worfolks' yard, which had three slipways, turned out 620 craft of all kinds before the brothers retired, both aged over ninety; among them were a number of these smacks, two-inch planked, with oak garboards, costing from £220 to £285.

After the decline of the oyster fishery referred to in Section three the largest smacks were chiefly employed on whelking. Whelks in the Wash were exhausted around 1875, after which the smacks had to voyage ten to twenty miles offshore to the Dowsing and Dudgeon Sands, sailing on Sunday evenings and returning on Fridays, with one craft bringing home the catch at mid-week. They towed heavy fifteen-foot boats from which shanks of pots, thirty pots to the shank, were set between anchors. Fishing was in water as deep as ten fathoms, and the shanks were hauled by hand. As there were always two pots off the ground at any time, it was heavy work, and the grounds were known as The Pull.

Crabs, which were put aside by the shrimpers and known as "swinnies", were the best bait; when they were not available fish offal or even horse meat was used. The heavy boats, too big to be carried on deck, were a constant problem in such turbulent waters, and often broke a four-inch bass tow rope when sheering in a seaway. But they needed to be seaworthy, for occasionally they failed to be picked up by the smack and had to fend for themselves. One with a cargo of whelks in her is said to have finished up in Yarmouth.

There is little evidence as to the antiquity of the whelk fishery, nor is it clear whether the "beehive" pot used is of earlier origin than the "bird cage" crab pot, only introduced on the East Coast in the eighteen-sixties.

The smaller smacks, up to fifty feet, trawled for prawns, as pink shrimps were locally described. The twenty-foot beam trawls were hauled by hand without winch or capstan. A net heavy with prawns was got alongside and the contents divided into "cuts" to be got on deck, though the King's Lynn boats (which in the last twenty years of the trade came to outnumber those from Boston) rigged a masthead tackle known as a "Jackson's Patent".

123

The Lynn shrimper

THE INSHORE fishing boats of the Wash, unlike the Essex oyster dredgers, were not small-scale replicas of the offshore smacks. They were of quite a different form, having long flat counter sterns, a narrow beam and a peculiarly sharp, lean bow. Up to forty feet long, they were pole-masted with the masts set well inboard about one third of the boat's length abaft the stem, and set a high-peaked mainsail. Usually one-and-a-half-inch planked, they were undecked amidships for convenience in carrying cockles and mussels, an occupation often more important than the trade from which they took their name. Instead of the full-width handspike anchor windlasses used by the smacks, they were content with short ratchet barrels set between the bitts.

These half-deckers also worked out of most of the Wash inlets, including Fosdyke where there were eleven and Sutton Bridge where there were four or five, and thus needed to be very handy to negotiate the narrow channels leading to their fishing grounds. For this reason they had heavily raked sternposts, and probably it was considered that the fine lines of the bow also helped.

For shrimping they employed two trawls, an eight-foot beam worked forward and a twelve worked aft, each on a bridle. When the time came to haul,

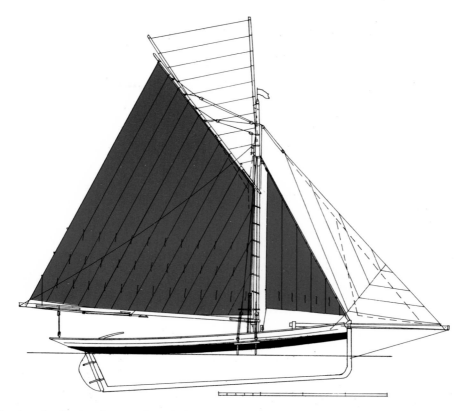

the headsail was dropped and the small net hauled till the bridle block could be slipped over a thole pin in the rail. As the shrimper rode to this the larger net was hauled up before the small one was got on deck. A tell-tale beam trawl, a pretty little miniature model, was carried to detect shrimps. The shrimp trawls were also used for fishing soles in season, with pockets laced to the sides, and a "tickler chain" rigged between the trawl heads in front of the ground rope of the net to stir the fish.

Mussels and cockles were raked entirely by hand, with the smack dried out, as noted in the description of the Leigh cockler, but with the rake head limited to one foot in width, and with a minimum of three-quarters of an inch between the teeth. The boats were thus used solely for transport. Several Lynn shrimpers, unrigged and motorised, and often with their long counters cut short as the result of damage or decay, survive to this day in the Fisher Fleet, their owners having been less disposed than most fishermen to replace them with more up-to-date craft, and sometimes having found it uneconomic to do so. These include *Queen Alexandra*, built by Worfolks, and on the evidence of the old regatta racing the fastest of them all.

The remaining outlet to the Wash and its fishing grounds, Wisbech also had a fleet of cutters about thirty feet long but, unlike the Lynn boats of similar size, they were fitted with full-width anchor windlasses.

The Norfolk and Suffolk class lifeboat

ALTHOUGH the north-east coast developed the first effective pulling lifeboat, it was an Essex coachbuilder, Lionel Lukin, who was probably the pioneer designer in this field, and it fell to East Anglia to build the first powerful long-range sailing lifeboat. This became known everywhere as the Norfolk and Suffolk type.

In the days of sail, great fleets funnelled down the North Sea towards London. Offshore sandbanks produced dangerous hazards for them at all times and, in gale force winds, heavy breaking seas. A particularly sturdy and weatherly lifeboat was required to withstand these conditions and carry out long-distance rescue work for vessels in distress.

The class varied in size between thirty-four and forty-six feet overall, and the largest had a beam of twelve feet. Heavily built and with an almost flat bottom, they were well suited for work in shallow seas. In addition to a heavy iron keel, they were equipped with sub-divided water ballast arrangements. The anchor and cable were shipped in a well amidships, where they served as additional ballast, producing, together with a generous beam, an extremely stable boat. They were however unlikely to right themselves in the event of a capsize, but this was a failing which their volunteer crews were prepared to accept.

Unlike the self-righting lifeboats, with their cork-like buoyancy, the greater weight of the clinker-built Norfolk and Suffolk boats enabled them to smash through rather than ride over a heavy sea, and inevitably they shipped a great deal of water. This was dealt with by more than a score of large relieving valves and tubes discharging through the bottom of the boat and by scupper-holes through each side, above the exceptionally broad belting of canvas-covered cork.

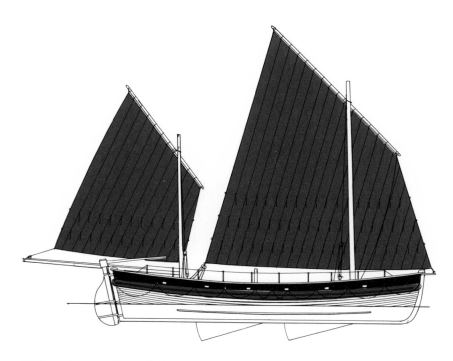

All but the smallest of them were difficult to manage under oars alone, and so the class might be said to have been a long-range sailing one, with its sail plan derived from the beach yawls. This was a massive spread of canvas, compared with other types of lifeboat, and required two large drop keels to provide lateral resistance. Like the beach yawls, they were built locally by Beeching, J. Critten, and Mills and Blake, while the improved model, of which the Aldeburgh *City of Winchester* was the finest example, was launched by the Thames Iron Works at Millwall.

In the days of sail, there were over thirty lifeboat stations along the length of the East Anglian coast, so that a crew would, with luck, be able to render assistance to a vessel which was down wind of their base. The R.N.L.I. was dependent upon earning and retaining the confidence of the beachmen who manned their boats. Evidence of this is provided by the development of another class of lifeboat peculiar to the East Anglian seaboard, the Cromer type.

In 1884 the Cromer men voted strongly for a new boat which was of the non-self-righting type. The new boat which they strongly approved of was thirty-five feet in length and pulled fourteen oars. It was virtually an improved version of the North Country type of lifeboat used at Cromer between 1804 and 1858, and was modestly rigged with two standing lugs and a foresail, but worked largely under oars. Later stations at Blakeney and Wells were supplied with similar, but slightly beamier, boats. The last East Coast sailing lifeboat is preserved at nearby Sheringham. She is the *Henry Ramey Upcher*, built in 1894 on the lines of a Sheringham fishing boat, and is to be seen at her home station as a worthy reminder of the heroic days of rescue under sail and oar.

The Revenue cutter

THROUGHOUT the eighteenth century and the first quarter of the nineteenth, the Revenue cutters were the proudest, as well as the most feared, of local craft. Their only rivals must have been the Naval cutters and the Harwich North Sea packets, which were also cutters of eighty to a hundred tons, usually about seventy feet long with nineteen feet beam.

A "Wivenhoe smack" was employed by the Customs as early as 1698, though surprisingly Harwich was not so provided till thirty years later. Both places then saw a succession of cutters, each larger than its predecessor, in a continual and usually unsuccessful effort to keep pace with the ever-increasing strength of the smuggling craft against which they were pitted.

The sixty-ton *Walpole*, built at Ipswich for the Harwich station in 1726, was a typical example of the period—fifty-four feet overall by sixteen feet eight inches beam with a depth of seven feet six inches. Plans were produced, but the local Commander asked that she be "fuller than the draft, both fore and aft, being frequently under water in a grown sea which commonly run short"—a picturesque way of explaining the sort of hull needed for the steep chops of the North Sea. She was replaced by a succession of cutters named *Argus* and *Bee*. The first *Argus* was of sixty-eight tons, and the third, built in 1777, of 133 tons, with a crew of twenty-four. Her successor, the fourth to bear the name, carried

ROGER FINCH

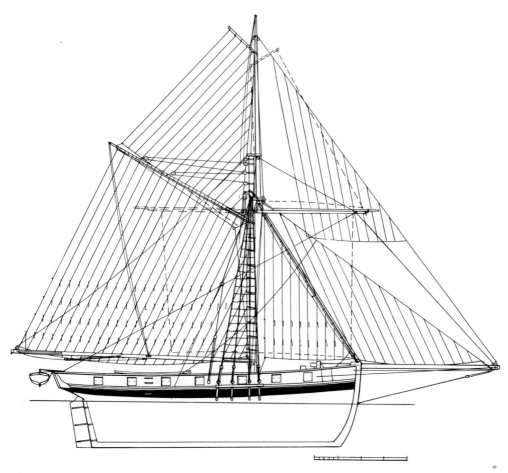

fourteen carronades, yet was overpowered and captured in 1807 by a sixty-ton French lugger with a crew of sixty, also mounting fourteen guns.

The later Colne cutters, based on Wivenhoe, bore the name *Repulse*. The first, built in 1774, had a crew of only eleven, but the sixth in 1793 was of 143 tons with a crew of thirty-seven. With increasing size, clinker planking was replaced by carvel, the change dating probably from around 1780.

At Yarmouth the cutters bore the name *Hunter*. One of these was lost with all hands off Winterton in 1807. The port of Maldon, which for administrative purposes then extended from Mersea to a point opposite Gravesend, had no Customs cutter, but Bradwell was the base for one of the cutters of the separate fleet owned by the Excise, then an independent department.

Reforms of the Preventive service in the 1820s decreased the number and importance of the Revenue cutters, whose duties and crews were largely transferred to stationary watch vessels, which had small cruising tenders but relied largely on boat patrols. Naval lieutenants were appointed to command the remaining cutters in 1831, though an exception was made for one specially respected Harwich Customs Commander, Isaac Saxby, who was appointed to command the *Scout* as late as 1841. Before his time, in 1814, the *Scout* won a race organised to test the sailing qualities of the cutters. Six craft competed from Harwich round the Cork and Kentish Knock lightvessels to Margate—an event one would have liked to have witnessed. Another of the latter-day Harwich "cutters", the eighty-one-ton *Viper*, probably owned by the Excise (built at Cowes in 1805 and paid off in 1817) was, unusually, schooner-rigged, as were some of the Naval so-called cutters.

After the introduction of the coastguard in the 1820s and the decline of smuggling the remaining cutters came to regard the salvage of wrecks as their main occupation, and after the institution of lifeboats in the middle of the century they chiefly served to occupy members of the Naval Reserve. One of the last survivors was the thirty-ton cutter *Snipe*, which lay on a mooring among the oyster smacks at West Mersea throughout the first decade of the twentieth century. Her handling was regarded by the smacksmen with the derision inevitably reserved for brassbound Navy men, till she was towed away shortly before the First World War, only to sink when she reached The Gat, between the North East Gunfleet and the West Rocks. The last Bradwell Revenue cruiser, *Mermaid,* built as a steamer in 1853 but converted to sail two years later, was still remembered there half a century ago.

The miniature spritsail barge *Cygnet,* built at Frindsbury in 1881, berthed in Frog Alley on the Orwell. She is still afloat as a yacht barge based at Pin Mill.   *A. Lambert*

Museums

THE PERMANENT preservation of any craft, indeed of any artefact, requires protection from wind and weather. The Dutch have shown how this can be done with a superb conversion of old waterside warehouses at Enkhuizen, housing fully rigged tjalks and botters, an example not even considered when during the nineteen-eighties hundreds of millions of pounds were spent on turning derelict docks into residential and commercial centres in London and other cities.

The next best form of conservation is active employment, even if in occupations very different from those for which a vessel was built. The Passmore Edwards Museum at Stratford, London, has shown an interesting initiative in keeping the sailing barge *Dawn*, built at Maldon in 1897, under sail. Another barge, the *Cambria*, was acquired by the Maritime Trust and lay for some years in St Katharine's Dock, London, but with the dispersal of the Trust's collection there she was moved to the Dolphin Yard, a lively working barge museum at Sittingbourne in Kent.

The Colchester oyster smack *Shramrock* is among the big collection of craft, chiefly foreign, at Exeter Maritime Museum, where she has been named the *TSW Shamrock* (in recognition of the contribution of Television South West to her preservation). She is happily kept alive by the sailing club associated with the Museum. At Sheringham the lifeboat *Henry Ramey Upcher*, built in 1894, is now preserved by the local council.

At Great Yarmouth Norfolk Museums have established the Maritime Museum for East Anglia at the old Shipwrecked Sailors' Home opened in 1859. The exhibits include a collection of relics and models that accumulated in the building in its days as a sailors' home. While it can hardly yet be said to cover East Anglia, it admirably illustrates the Norfolk ports and waterways. At Lowestoft there is an unpretentious but fascinating collection at the museum at Sparrow's Nest brought together and maintained by the Lowestoft and East Suffolk Maritime Society. The nucleus was originally displayed in a typical flint-built cottage. Now enlarged, it provides an unequalled opportunity for the visitor to gain an insight into the port's fishing industry under sail and steam as well as much else associated with East Coast sail. It stands as an example to be followed by other small ports with a tradition of sail and oar.

Southwold has its Fishermen's Reading Room, founded in 1863, overlooking the North Sea. It holds a number of models, among them miniatures of the beach boats and other relics of the town's seagoing past. Aldeburgh Museum, in the ancient Moot Hall, contains models and nautical relics which it is hoped will one day be brought together to provide a coherent record of the port's history.

Glossary

This glossary is largely confined to words and phrases which are peculiar to the East Anglian seaboard and waterways. Words with a much wider currency have only been included when they provide a guide for the general reader.

A-croke, lying	Lying hove-to hand-lining, with the headsails lowered, while the main and mizzen booms are guyed out to leeward.
Admiral	An experienced skipper in charge of a group of sailing trawlers in the days of fleeting (q.v.).
Backer-in	The fisherman who coils down long lines.
Barge-built	A method of constructing a wooden hull, flat-bottomed, without an external keel and with a hard chine. The seams are generally made watertight by a rabbeted joint and treated with a flexible compound of tar and animal hair; alternatively a double skin was used, similarly treated between the two layers of planking.
Barking	Preserving canvas sails with a mixture of cutch, oak bark tannin and oil.
Barm skin	Oilcloth apron worn by herring fishermen when hauling the nets in order to keep fish scales, etc. from their clothing. Originally a leather apron.
Baulks	Beams spreading open the top and bottom of the mouth of a stowboat net.
Bawley	Transom-sterned, cutter-rigged fishing boat with a boomless mainsail. When used for shrimping, they carried boilers aboard for treating the catch and it is possible that the name derives from this practice, i.e. "boiler-boat".
Beatsters	Men or women engaged ashore in mending fishing nets.
Big mizzener	Dandy (q.v.) with the mizzen stepped forward of the rudder head and thus strictly a ketch.
Blobs	Jelly fish.
Boaked	Used to describe the hatches of a Norfolk wherry when they are raised to accommodate a bulky cargo.
Bonnet	An additional piece of sail canvas attached to the foot of the sail by lacings.
Boomie	A barge-built vessel fitted with a gaff and boom rig.
Bottles	The glass floats fitted to a drift net or to a trawl headline.
Bowdle	Fisherman's apron.
Breaming	Burning off marine growth from a vessel's bottom and simultaneously liquifying the tar to facilitate scraping. Bunches of reeds or straw were used, held in a long-handled breaming hook.

132

Brood	Oysters up to three years old.
Brumagen pilot	An unlicensed pilot, usually a local fisherman who would assist a merchant vessel in a strange river.
Bumkin	Short iron bowsprit, but frequently used in conjunction with a conventional wooden one; also a small, open sailing boat often fitted in this way. On River Colne decked, transom-sterned smack.
Cant	The edge of an offshore clay shelf, exposed at low water.
Chocker pole	Short topmast, also known as chockstaff, set up at the head of a smack's mast in winter; largely for appearance's sake, but occasionally a small topsail was set on it.
Chopstick	See sprawl.
Codbanger	Cod-fishing vessel or the men who sailed aboard it, from the practice of knocking cod on the head with a club before they were sent to market.
Cod end	The tail end of a trawl, or similar net, in which the catch was retained until emptied on deck.
Codling	Small cod, less than a standard length, which was usually about two feet.
Cran	A measurement of volume equal to approximately one thousand herring.
Convertor smack	Fishing sailing vessels, popular at Lowestoft at the end of the nineteenth century. They could, with the minimum of difficulty, be rigged and fitted out for either trawling or herring driftnet fishing.
Corft	Floating chest to store live cod or lobsters until required for the market (Harwich).
Cotchell cargo	One made up of several different consignments, each to be delivered to a different merchant.
Crome	Tool used for lifting septaria stone aboard a smack and having three curved prongs at the foot of the staff. Hence, crome-nosed, to describe a vessel with a curved stem.
Culch (cultch)	Clean shell or similar material spread on the oyster grounds to receive the spat during the spawning season.
Cultac	Blunt, dagger-shaped knife used by oystermen for separating clusters of small oysters, removing nuns (q.v.), etc.
Dandy	Yawl-rigged (in the modern sense) (q.v.) produced in the first instances by reducing the length of a cutter's main boom and stepping a short mizzen mast.
Dickie-rigged	Ketch-rigged (Norfolk and northwards).
Didel or dydel	A net attached to an iron hoop, mounted on an ash staff to pick up fish dropped as a net comes inboard. Also used for removing oysters from pits, shrimps from boilers, etc.
Doble	The version of the peter boat (q.v.) used on the River Medway.
Dole	The share claimed by a longshoreman when his company's boat was involved in a salvage claim.
Dredge (vb)	To employ a special technique to maintain control of direction when a sailing vessel was drifting with the tide. By dropping the anchor so that it dragged over the bottom, a differential between the speed of the tide and that of the vessel was produced, enabling the vessel to answer the helm.

Dredge (n)	A triangle of wrought iron to which, at its apex, a towing rope is attached. The base is fitted with a hoeing edge for gathering oysters, scallops or mussels into the strongly woven net which is lashed to the dredge.
Drogues'l	A conical bag of canvas, whose mouth is extended with a steel hoop. It was used by smacks which towed it astern to reduce way when entering harbour.
Fastener	The act of coming fast when trawling as the net is caught on an obstruction; alt. the cause of it; in Essex, a fast.
Fives or Five fingers	Starfish, enemy of the oyster, once fished for agricultural fertiliser.
Flasket	Flat basket for carrying fish.
Flattie	A hard-chined rowing boat with a narrow transom stern, used on the North Norfolk coast and estuaries. Also known as a canoe or a flatbottom.
Floatum	Cromer name for a crab pot.
Gear	A vessel's sails, spars and rigging.
Hair and blair	A flexible sealing compound of cow, elk or horse hair, mixed with coal tar or cow dung and introduced between the joints of the planks when building a barge and between the two skins if a barge was doubled.
Half and halfer	Herring drifter whose earnings were divided equally between the owner and the crew.
Half-ware	Oysters between three and four years old. Oysters of marketable size were also known as ware.
Handfleets	Ropes connecting the ends of stowboat net baulks to the anchor chain, or cable, by way of the stringer.
Hazelling	Airing or drying fresh-caught shrimps before boiling.
Herring hole	A mortice slot cut in the top of a mast to accommodate a sheeve over which the halyard runs.
Hiplines	Tollesbury (Essex) name for a stowboater's templines (q.v.).
Hoodway	Companion leading down to the cabin.
Horse	A sand lying in mid-channel. Also a wooden or iron transverse beam across which the sheet of a sail works.
Hoveller	In Essex a man assisting sailing barges as an unofficial pilot and extra hand. In Norfolk a beach boat, a little larger than a crabber, whose crew were known as hovelleers.
Hoy barge	A craft making regular advertised passages with mixed cargoes and, in earlier times, passengers.
Huffler (hoveller, hubbler)	Man salvaging wrecks, recovering anchors, etc., or employed casually to assist in piloting or handling a vessel in narrow channels and under bridges. In Barking creek (Essex) called a dobber. Sometimes applied to small boats used in this work.
Jacksons's patent	Masthead tackle used by King's Lynn prawners for heaving the catch aboard.
Jenny Morgan	Wind vane popular on Norfolk wherries depicting a Welsh girl in silhouette. Later used to describe any of a number of wind vane designs.
Jigger	The large gaff topsail, usually of undressed canvas, used on a smack. A small mizzen.
Jigger yard	A stiffening to extend the foot of a gaff topsail, used on a smack.

Kevil or cavil rails	Stout pieces of timber fixed horizontally to the bulwark stanchions and to which halyards, sheets or trawl warps are belayed.
Kindle	The wind is said to kindle up when it starts to freshen.
Lab rake	Toothed rake and net on a long handle to catch mussels under water.
Little mizzener	A dandy rigged vessel with a small mizzen stepped abaft the rudder head.
Lute stern	An extension of a transom stern effected by wooden knees transversely boarded over for all or most of its underside.
Mast scuttle	Narrow slot in the deck, immediately aft of the mainmast, into which the mast fits when lowered; known as lears at Yarmouth.
Mitch board	Wooden crutch into which the mainmast was lowered when a sailing drifter lay to her nets; mitch lantern, a navigational light fixed to the top of the mitch board.
Mollygogger	A movable fairlead to accommodate the net warp of a fishing boat, fitted with both vertical and horizontal rollers. Its position could be altered to the most convenient station on the rail to suit the lead of the warp.
Mingle	Tool for dividing off the catch in the sleeve of a stowboat net into manageable sections.
Mulie	A barge-built (q.v.) vessel with a sprit-rigged mainmast and a mizzen setting a gaff sail, usually standing.
Nettles, knittles	Short lengths of line used to secure the head of a sail to its gaff or yard. Known also as rovings, robands or yardbands.
Norman	Short bar of wood, either oak or hickory, used to rotate the barrel of a windlass, usually "handspike".
Orruck	Oar port in Norfolk beach boat (presumably corruption of oarlock as in rowlock).
Peter boat	Small Thames fishing boat, used from above bridges down to Leigh and sometimes venturing as far as West Mersea; usually double-ended and spritsail-rigged. Name der. perhaps from the patron saint of fishermen, or perhaps from a church dedicated to him.
Peter net	Length of fishing net, usually caught and employed for stopping creeks; used by the peter boats (q.v.).
Pinion	Rope from cod end of stowboat net to smack's quarter.
Pink	In the early nineteenth century, a vessel built with a pointed stern, rigged in a variety of ways.
Pinker	Form of Norfolk beach boat, extinct by mid-nineteenth century. Presumably denoting a narrow pink stern.
Pinpatches	Winkles.
Pits	Shallow, steep sided rectangular pond to store oysters for market and protect them from frost in winter.
Planksheer (plancea)	The board which ran the length of a vessel, covering the heads of the frames and projecting a little beyond the main wale. Also covering board.
Poultering	Beachcombing (Suffolk).
Priddle	An oysterman's basket.
Quarter cran basket	Traditional wickerwork basket which was used for unloading herring at Lowestoft.

Raft	A bundle of spare spars, sweeps, quants, etc., usually accommodated in iron crutches set in the rail.
Rousing	Mixing salt with herrings.
Ruffle	Cast iron band in the centre of a windlass, notched so that the pawl can engage in it and prevent the barrel from rotating backwards. Also hole in the lower stem or fore gripe of a beach boat for attaching the recovery cable.
Sailorman	London River term which could refer to either a sailing barge or a member of its crew.
Salvaging	Assistance given to vessels wrecked or in distress and in particular the saving of their hulls, gear and cargo for reward.
Scroper	Harwich name for smack used for salvaging, or a man so employed.
Scudding	Clearing the herring nets at sea of fish over a pole above the fish hatch. In Essex, known as shaking out.
Seekers	Trading vessels which relied upon freights by fixing them themselves, as opposed to carrying cargoes of their owners' manufacture.
Shannock	A nickname for a Sheringham fisherman.
Sheards or shards	Two pieces of wood used by oystermen to assist in picking up rubbish from the deck of a smack when dredging.
Shoe-kettle	A metal welded kettle which could be inserted into the fire of a donkey engine on a smack to provide hot water for the galley.
Skeet	Wooden sleeper shod with an iron skid, or fitted with a roller and laid on a beach in order to run boats up and down. Vb. used to describe this operation.
Skillinger	Smack, usually from Brightlingsea, engaged in the deep-sea oyster fishery off Terschelling, Holland.
Slip	Small sole. The full classification, in order of size, was cats' tongues; slips, from 9½" to 10"; and soles, above 12".
Slob-up	To become choked with muddy silt or sand.
Smig	Undersized fish. Any small craft.
Snike, on the	Working on shares; also called sniking.
Snoods	Short lines for hooks to be attached on a handline or fastened at intervals on a long line.
Spat	Spawn of oysters, n. and vb. Also oysters up to one year old.
Spitfire	Small jib of heavy canvas.
Sprawl	The metal spreader which extended the two snoods of the handline.
Stocker or stocker bait	Small or unmarketable fish, usually a perquisite of the skipper and crew.
Stringer	Longitudinal strengthening member within a boat's hull, to brace her frames. Also short length of chain or wire connecting handfleets (q.v.) to the anchor chain or chain cable used when stowboating.
Stripe	Tall wicker basket, holding seven stone of mussels, used in the Wash.
Stumpie	A vessel of barge-build (q.v.), spritsail rigged but without a topmast, and only rarely with a bowsprit.
Sweeps	Long oars used for propelling a vessel in a calm, used aboard barges and fishing smacks.
Swills	Pannier-shaped baskets, used until recently at Yarmouth when landing herring.
Swimheader	A barge-built (q.v.) sailing vessel, with a shovel shaped bow or stern similar to a Thames lighter.
Swimmer	Sheringham name for a crab pot.

136

Swiping	Raising anchors lost in a roadstead by working over the ground with grapnels from boats.
Tabernacle	A three-sided wooden or metal box, mounted on deck or through deck to keel, to secure the foot of the mast and yet allow it to be lowered. The bargeman's mast case.
Tailing halyard	Device to lead a halyard of either the topsail or flying jib to the mainmast head and so relieve the strain on the topmast.
Templines	Vertical ropes by which the upper baulk of a stowboat net was suspended from the fore deck of the smack, one on each side.
Tendril or tindal, teendel	The oysterman's flat basket with a cross handle.
Tholes, or thole pins	Oak pegs fitted into holes in a boat's gunwale. Usually in pairs, with the oar working between them, but sometimes singly, with the oar held by a loose rope grommet.
Timber nogging	Post socketing in the stern bench of a stowboat smack to which the pinion (q.v.) was belayed.
Tinsing	A light caulk between planks.
Tingle	Mollusc which destroys young oysters by boring through their shell, whelk tingle or dog whelk (*Purpura lapillus*). Also rough patch nailed over a leak or other defect, often of lead or copper, sometimes backed by tarred felt, canvas or brown paper.
Tog	Undersized crab (Norfolk).
Tomboy	Wooden crook set in a hole in the cod smack rail with a notch in the outboard end to take the chafe of the handline.
Tommy Hunter	A stay leading forward from the mizzen masthead of a smack in order to tension the shrouds.
Tongue	Small sole.
Tonking post	Tollesbury name for timber nogging (q.v.).
Trim	A set net with a triangular mouth, used in the Wash estuaries.
Trim-tram	The old Leigh-on-Sea shrimp trawl having a net raised by a vertical upright stick mounted in the centre of the scraper board.
Trolleys	Wooden parrell balls, strung on a line to secure the gaff jaws to the mast.
Trolloper	Norfolk longshore shrimper.
Trotline	Inshore longline carrying snoods (q.v.) with hooks to catch fish, or threaded with bait without hooks, to catch whelks or eels.
Tub	An oysterman's measure, roughly the old Winchester bushel, just over twenty-one gallons.
Vangs	A pair of wires rigged from the sprit-end on a barge, one to either quarter and each fitted with a tackle known as the vang fall.
Wash	An oysterman's measure of volume, about five gallons.
Weagle lines	King's Lynn name for stowboater's templines. (q.v.)
Weather-cocked	The condition in which a vessel found herself when upon wending (q.v.) it lost way and lay head to wind.
Wells	Compartments in a smack's fish hold. Also a section of the bilge enclosed by bulkheads and open to the sea by means of small holes in the vessel's bottom; access obtained by a hatch on deck and a wooden trunk, the arrangement permitting fish to be carried alive.
Wend	To turn to windward; the point at which a sailing vessel goes on to the other tack and changes direction.

Wherry A name given to widely differing types of vessel; in the period covered by this book, it was reserved in East Anglia for a cargo-carrying vessel, almost entirely restricted to the Broads and its waterways.

Wim Lab rake (q.v.).

Windmill Accidental crossing of baulks when stowboat fishing.

Wink The fisherman's hand winch, on bawleys (q.v.) mounted on a single post and used for landing the trawl.

Winkle brig Name for small open sailing boat derived from the work for which they were usually used (West Mersea).

Withy Beacon marking edge of channel or oyster laying; usually a sapling driven into the mud.

Yarmouth Roads Roadstead off Great Yarmouth protected from easterly and north-easterly gales by the Scroby Sand; used as anchorage by large fleets awaiting fair wind or for refuge from bad weather in days of sail. Sailorman's term for the transverse locker at the after end of the cabin, across the transom. So named because for most spritsail barges, Yarmouth marked the limit of their trading area.

Yarmouth mittens Chapped hands.

Yawl In the modern sense, a two-masted sailing vessel with the mizzen mast stepped abaft the rudder head, but in the eighteenth century any small craft usually employed fishing, and in that sense it survived until recently at Whitstable to describe cutter-rigged smacks. In the Wash, yoll signifies a double-ended cutter-rigged cockle and mussel boat.

Yoll See yawl.

The miniature spritsail barge *Cygnet* under way in Harwich harbour in the nineteen-thirties.
A. Lambert

Bibliography

General

Anson, P. *Fishermen and Fishing Ways*. George G. Harrap, 1932.

Arnott, W. G. *Suffolk Estuary*. [River Deben]. Norman Adlard, Ipswich, 1950.

Arnott, W. G. *Alde Estuary*. Norman Adlard, Ipswich, 1952.

Arnott, W. G. *Orwell Estuary*. Norman Adlard, Ipswich, 1954.

Benham, H. *Last Stronghold of Sail*. George G. Harrap, 1947; reprinted 1986.

Benham, H. *Once Upon a Tide*. George G. Harrap, 1955; reprinted 1986.

Bottomley, A. F. *A Short History of the Borough of Southwold*. Southwold Corporation, 1974.

Carr, F. and Mason, F. *Vanishing Craft*. Country Life, 1934.

Carter, F. *Looming Lights*. Constable, 1947.

Cooke, E. W. *Shipping and Craft*. 1829; reprinted with commentary by Roger Finch, Masthead, 1970.

Cooper, E. R. *A Suffolk Coast Garland*. Heath Cranton, 1928.

Cooper, E. R. *Mardles from Suffolk*. Heath Cranton, 1932.

Cooper, E. R. *Storm Warriors of the Suffolk Coast*. Heath Cranton, 1937.

Copping, A. E. *Gotty and the Guv'nor*. E. Grant Richards, 1907; republished, Mallard Reprints, 1979.

Dickin, E. P. *History of Brightlingsea*. D. H. James, Brightlingsea, 1939.

Finch, R. *Sailing Craft of the British Isles*. Collins, 1976.

Finch, R. *The Pierhead Painters*. Barrie & Jenkins, 1983.

Frost, E. J. *From Tree to Sea*. Terence Dalton, 1985.

Hedges, A. A. C. *East Coast Shipping*. Shire Publications, 1974.

Hughes, B. C. *History of Harwich Harbour*. Harwich Harbour Conservancy Board, 1939.

Leather, J. *Gaff Rig*. Adlard Coles, 1970.

McKee, E. *Working Boats of Britain*. Conway Maritime Press, 1983.

Malster, R. *Wreck and Rescue on the Essex Coast*. D. Bradford Barton, 1968.

Malster, R. *Saved from the Sea*. Terence Dalton, 1974.

Pipe, J. *Port on the Alde*. [Snape]. Snape Craft Shop, 1976.

Steers, J. A. *The Sea Coast*. Collins, 3rd edition, 1962.

Thompson, L. *Smugglers of the Suffolk Coast*. Boydell Press, Ipswich, 1968.

White, E. W. *British Fishing Boats and Coastal Craft*, Parts 1 and 2. H.M.S.O., 1973.

Wren, W. J. *Ports of the Eastern Counties*. Terence Dalton, 1976.

Traders under Sail

Allendale, J. *Sailorman between the Wars*. J. Hallewell, 1978.

Benham, H. *Down Tops'l*. George G. Harrap, 1951; reprinted 1986.

Benham, H. *The Salvagers*. Essex County Newspapers, 1980.

Benham, H. & Finch, R. *The Big Barges*. George G. Harrap, 1983.

Bennett, A. S. *Us Bargemen*. Meresborough Books, 1980.

Carr, F. *Sailing Barges*. Revised edition, Conway Maritime Press, 1971.

Clark, R. *Black Sailed Traders*. Putnam, 1961.

Cooper, F. S. *A Handbook of Sailing Barges*. Adlard Coles, 1955.

Cooper, F. S. *Racing Sailormen*. Percival Marshall, 1963.

Finch, R. *Coals from Newcastle*. Terence Dalton, 1973.

Finch, R. *A Cross in the Topsail*. Boydell Press, Ipswich, 1979.

Horlock, A. H. & R. J. *Mistleyman's Log*. Fisher Nautical Press, 1977.
Horsley, J. *Tools of the Maritime Trades*. David and Charles, 1978.
Ionides, C. *A Floating Home*. Chatto & Windus, 1918.
Kemp, J. *A Fair Wind for London*. Sailtrust, 1983.
Malster, R. *Wherries and Waterways*. Terence Dalton, 1971; revised 1986.
Martin, E. G. *Sailorman*. Oxford University Press, 1933, 1950.
Roberts, A. W. *Coasting Bargemaster*. Edward Arnold, 1949; revised edition Terence Dalton, 1984.
Roberts, A. W. *Last of the Sailormen*. Routledge & Kegan Paul, 1960.
Uglow, J. *Sailorman—A Bargemaster's Story*. Conway Maritime Press, 1975.

Fishing

Benham, H. *The Stowboaters*. Essex County Newspapers, 1977.
Benham, H. *The Codbangers*. Essex County Newspapers, 1979.
Boswell, D. *The Fishing Log of Edwin Smith, 1884–8*. Grimsby Public Libraries and Museum, 1969.
Buckland, F. *The Fisheries of Norfolk*. 1875.
Bulstrode, H. T. *Report on Shell Fisheries*. Ministry of Agriculture and Fisheries, 1909.
Butcher, D. *The Driftermen*. Tops'l Books, 1979.
Butcher, D. *The Trawlermen*. Tops'l Books, 1980.
Clark, R. *The Longshoremen*. David and Charles, 1974.
Collard, A. E. *The Oyster and Dredgermen of Whitstable*. Joseph Collard, 1902.
Dade, E. *Sail and Oar*. J. M. Dent, 1933.
Davis, F. M. *An Account of the Fishing Gear of England and Wales*. Ministry of Agriculture & Fisheries, Fishery Investigations, 1923, 1927, 1932, 1958.
Elder, J. *The Royal Fishing Companies*. 1911.
Elliot, C., & Jenkins, F. *Sailing Fishermen in Old Photographs*. Tops'l Books, 1978.
Franklin, *The Crab and its Fisheries*. Fisheries Laboratory, Burnham-on-Crouch, 1972.
Festing, S. *Fishermen*. David & Charles, 1977.
Frost, M. *Boadicea CK213*. Angus & Robertson, 1974.
Frost, M. *Half a Gale*. K. Mason, 1981.
Holdsworth, E. W. *Deep Sea Fishing and Fishing Boats*. 1874.
Leather, J. *The Northseamen*. Terence Dalton, 1971.
Leather, J. *The Salty Shore*. [River Blackwater]. Terence Dalton, 1975.
Leather, M. *Saltwater Village*. [Rowhedge]. Terence Dalton, 1977.
March, E. J. *Sailing Drifters*. Percival Marshall, 1952; reprinted by David and Charles, 1969.
March, E. J. *Sailing Trawlers*. Percival Marshall, 1953; reprinted by David and Charles, 1969.
March, E. J. *Inshore Craft of Britain in the Days of Sail and Oar*, Vols 1 & 2. David and Charles, 1970.
Mather, E. J. *Nor'ard of the Dogger*. James Nisbet, 1888.
Murie, J. *Thames Estuary Sea Fisheries*. Waterlow Bros & Layton, 1903.
Samuel, A. M. *The Herring*. John Murray, 1918.
Stibbons, P., Lee, K. and Warren, M. *Crabs and Shannocks*. Poppyland Publishing, Cromer, 1983.
Warren, P. J. *The Fishery for the Pink Shrimp in the Wash*. Fishery Laboratory, Lowestoft, 1973.

General Index

Index of Places and Ships' Names

References to illustrations are in **bold type**, s.b. indicates sailing barge.

Index of Personal Names

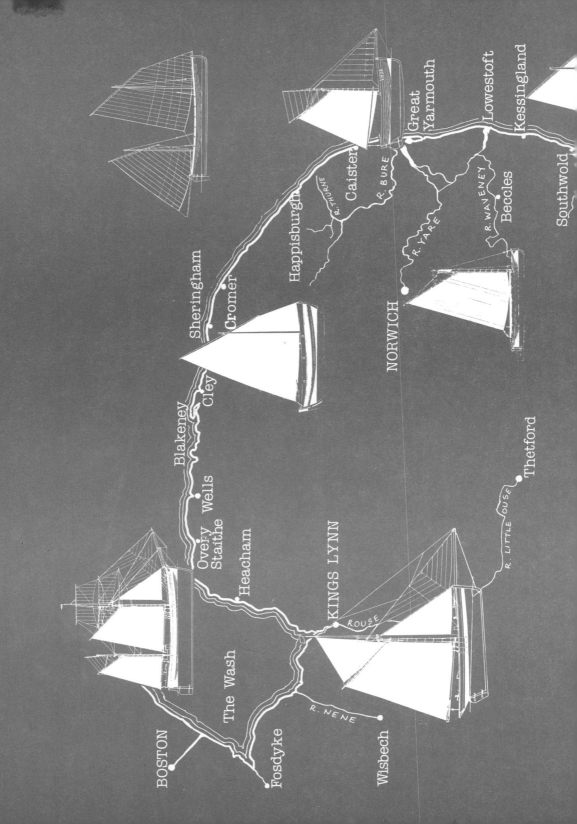

BOSTON

Fosdyke

The Wash

Heacham

Overy
Staithe

Wells

Blakeney

Cley

Sheringham

Cromer

Happisburgh

R. THURNE

Caister

R. BURE

Great
Yarmouth

Lowestoft

Kessingland

Southwold

R. YARE

R. WAVENEY

Beccles

NORWICH

KINGS LYNN

ROUSE

R. NENE

Wisbech

R. LITTLE OUSE

Thetford